# SOCA BABY

**For the entire soca community:
the lovers of soca, the children of soca,
the artists, DJs, producers, and all the
carnival chasers.**

**And a special thank you to Ras Shorty I**

**This book was inspired by our children and the sweet melody of soca.**



First Published in Brooklyn, NY, USA by Water Lily Publishing
ISBN: 979-8-9903099-0-6
Library of Congress Control Number: 2024906209
www.waterlilypublishing.com

Ariful Mowla Qef Johnson

# SOCA BABY

# Soca Baby

is a bundle of joy

Born to parents who

LOVE SOCA, oh boy!

Soca Baby
SHAKES TO THE
BEAT

Moves those tiny feet
oh so sweet!

Soca Baby

loves **BRIGHT** colors

WEARS A

ONESIE AND BACKPACK

LIKE NO OTHER

Soca Baby Smiles

and spreads

HAPPY CHEER

Soca Baby's laughter rings out

LOUD and CLEAR

Soca Baby
loves to sing
sings to the beat

and drums on
EVERYTHING

Soca Baby
dances and twirls

Soca Baby moves
in soca swirls

Soca Baby
LOVES

soca's Caribbean roots
with sunshine, beaches
and tropical fruits

**Soca Baby**
**knows how to play**

From sunrise
to sunset
EVERYDAY

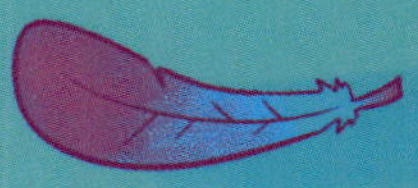

Soca Baby's

spirit is sweet

and FREE

a little

WARRIOR

full of energy

# Soca Baby IS FULL OF PRIDE

the love for LIFE
Soca Baby will never hide

Soca Baby

you're one of a kind

Your love for soca

will be forever enshrined

# Soca Baby

keep shining bright

You're a true

SOCA STAR

in every right!

Manufactured by Amazon.ca
Bolton, ON

40814368R00017

# FIRESIDE CHATS

## (VOLUME ONE)

Future Pathways

TakingITGlobal
INSPIRE INFORM INVOLVE

# CONTENTS

TakingITGlobal
117 Peter Street, Suite 212
Toronto, Ontario
M5V 0M3



ISBN: 978-0-578-32176-9 (paperback)

Produced with the financial support of the Government of Canada's
Supports for Student Learning program

Cover and unit illustrations by Shaikara David, Akwesasne Mohawk Territory

**www.firesidechats.ca**

# CHRISTINE M'LOT

| | |
|---|---|
| CAREER | Activism |
| IDENTITY | First Nations |
| PROVINCE/TERRITORY | Manitoba |

*Written by Jasmine Kabatay*

Since she was a child, Christine M'Lot knew when she grew up she wanted to be a teacher. From Swan Lake First Nation, but born and raised in Winnipeg, Manitoba, M'Lot says she was really lucky she always knew she wanted to work with children, and that school was something she always liked and helped her out a lot.

*"I even used to make my little sister be my student and I would teach her things and give her homework, which probably really sucked for her, but it was fun for me,"* said M'Lot.

Of course she couldn't just head straight to the classroom, she had to learn how to teach. So she went to the University of Winnipeg for a five-year program, where she was part of an integrated program.

The integrated program meant not only was she learning what she wanted to teach, but they also have to pick a teachable major and a minor, so what subject areas they want to teach.

For M'Lot, she says what she really liked about her program was that they were in classrooms and for placements she was there to observe and get a feel of what kind of class she would like to teach. From there, she knew she wanted to be a high school teacher.

M'Lot teaches English for students in grades 9–11, as well as a grade 12 global issues course and a mandatory grade nine truth and reconciliation course, which she says students are shocked to learn about the history.

*"Oftentimes, their middle years education kind of consists of all the nice things about Indigenous topics and they don't really get into the hard truth yet,"* said M'Lot.

She says she also tries to make aspects of the course positive, such as Indigenous contributions to society and teaches them aspects about her culture as well because students would be sad when leaving the classroom.

*Illustration by Kailey Sheppard*

Even though she is teaching students and is doing what she loves, M'Lot faced many personal obstacles to get where she is today.

She went through a difficult time in high school, and started acting out and falling into a negative lifestyle of drugs and alcohol.

*"Addiction runs in my family and so I always kind of grew up thinking like, 'Oh, I'm never going to be like that.'"*

M'Lot was really close to not being able to graduate and become a teacher, until her boyfriend started getting her to think about her choices and what she really wanted in life.

*"He noticed that I was doing all these stupid things and he's like, 'Why are you getting drunk every weekend? Why are you doing this? You want to be a teacher.' And he really helped me get on a good track,"* said M'Lot.

She said the questions he asked her and the things he said to her were really powerful and *"exactly"* what she needed in that moment.

Now, she tells youth who may encounter similar things she went through to stick to who you are and to always remember your goals, and says it was really important for her to be a teacher because she has always had that end goal and was something she knew she wanted to do.

*"Stick to your goals and surround yourself with people who are doing the types of things that you want to do. Don't surround yourself with people who are going to be negative influences on you,"* said M'Lot.

And if there's one thing she can tell people, and she tells this to her students all the time, it would be: do things now that your future self will thank you for.

*Watch the Future Pathways Fireside Chats video interview with Christine at https://www.firesidechats.ca/video/christine-mlot*

# DAKOTA BEAR

| | |
|---|---|
| CAREER | Activism |
| IDENTITY | First Nations |
| PROVINCE/TERRITORY | British Columbia |

*Written by Jessica Dee Humphreys*

Dakota Bear is a 26-year old hip hop artist, land protector, warrior entrepreneur, clothing designer, business consultant, motivational speaker, and youth mentor from the Treaty 6 Territory. His copious interests speak to his energy and passion; and, in every one of his many endeavours, Dakota brings his Indigenous identity to the forefront.

*"Whether I'm writing a song or creating a project, I'm always thinking about who is listening to it, and what they are getting from it.... inspiration really does come from our Indigenous culture."*

This is what Dakota's role as a warrior entrepreneur is all about: *"Taking the values of our Indigenous culture and bringing those to our businesses: carrying ourselves in a good way, giving back to the community, ensuring that we're only taking what we need."* Dakota builds all of his enterprises with this noble ethic, and also provides advice to other Indigenous businesses.

Though Dakota has been making music for 10 years, it was only after attending a business course in Vancouver that he found a way to pursue his passion further, *"not only as a hobby or something I did to feed my creative side, but something that I was able to have as a career path."*

Dakota was able to apply the lessons he learned about publicity, marketing, and all aspects of business management to his other ventures, too. *"Having that education greatly helped me. I learned so much within that eight month programme."* But Dakota also learned a lot from less formal sources, as well: *"[I was] doing online courses anywhere that I could, that had Indigenous instructors online or videos, and how-to tutorials. And then taking that knowledge...and using that to help launch [a] business."*

Dakota's work is not only about creating, but also sharing. *"With the platforms I have, I'm hoping to spread messages of hope to young Indigenous peoples, also spread truth and awareness on issues that we face as Indigenous people, whether that be through my music, or through the clothing that me and my partner design, or speaking more directly at schools....just using the platforms we have created over the years to really empower and inspire younger people."*

Dakota's motivation to guide and inspire others likely stems from the mentorships and guidance that he received when he was young and struggling. *"When my father left, my uncles took the role of wanting to teach me things that I needed to learn growing up as a young man. Just to have those people as mentors in my life, those family members, helped me greatly."*

Sadly, one of Dakota's uncles passed away in 2016. Losing him helped Dakota further understand the important role his uncle had played in Dakota's life. *"It made me realize that it's important to have somebody there...And that's why I'm so dedicated to helping young people...It's kind of like reciprocal."*

Dakota describes his younger self as *"spending so much time caught up in the wrong things... messing around, wasting time, partying and drinking."* It was many years before he came to the realization that he was behaving this way because he was *"coping in an unhealthy way with intergenerational trauma."*

Dakota defines the meaning behind this powerful term: *"'Intergenerational trauma' is feeling the effects of the pass and permit system, residential schools, the 60's scoop and more, feeling the trauma of these plights that our grandparents and our parents had felt without actually going through that ourselves. We carry that through our blood, we carry it through our DNA. The trauma can get attached in that way."*

Living with an absentee father, a mother battling additions, and other family members struggling with alcoholism, Dakota sought to find positive examples similarly carried through his Indigenous bloodline.

*"It is also knowing that we're very resilient. Through the 500 years of colonialism that we have been faced with, through all the adversities and the plights, through all of this, we're still here. We're still thriving. We're still growing. We're still learning our culture. We're still learning our languages. And it's really knowing that we are able to grow and we are able to move forward."*

*Illustration by Shaikara David*

Today, Dakota lives in Vancouver, pursuing his many interests — music, videos, design, youth education, business, and raising awareness about Indigenous land and rights — as well as being a loving, full-time partner and father. He and his family use their culture to keep connected and grounded, through prayer, smudging, giving thanks, and spending time on the land. *"Things that are really positive and feed us, feed our spirits."*

Dakota knows that many Indigenous youth may be faced with the fallout from intergenerational trauma, and his message — like his music — is for them.

*"I wish I could have been more self aware when I was younger. I wish I could have spent more time understanding those things, talking with counsellors, healing from those things. I'm doing it now. It's not too late. I'm 26, and that's okay. Took me some time to learn. I hurt myself along the way and I made mistakes along the way. But I've grown from those things."*

*"And so I guess my advice would just be take care of yourself and make sure that if you have some things that are weighing on your chest and you're going through some stuff, there's healthy ways to deal with those things. You can learn from them, you can grow, and become a very strong person... Make sure that you have a good support system and... you're always expressing yourself and letting that out, not bottling it up. And make sure that you're always [aiming to be] healthy and happy."*

**Freedom, by Dakota Bear**

*"You'll hear us off in the distance/*

*We are the kids that you dismissed/*

*We are the targets you just missed/*

*We are descendent of healers and chiefs/*

*Just know that our struggles are brief....*

*We are the warriors!"*

*Watch the Future Pathways Fireside Chats video interview with Dakota at https://www.firesidechats.ca/video/dakota-bear*

# REANNA MERASTY

| | |
|---|---|
| CAREER | Architecture |
| IDENTITY | First Nations |
| PROVINCE/TERRITORY | Manitoba |

*Written by Jasmine Kabatay*

Reanna Merasty has an impressive resume under her belt. From Barren Lands First Nation, but grew up mostly in Brandon, Manitoba, she is working in the field of architecture and design. Merasty holds a Bachelor of Environmental Design and is working on her Masters of Architecture at the University of Manitoba.

Not only this, but she works as a student intern and designer at Brook McIlroy in their Indigenous design studio and as a research assistant on several housing projects. Though what exposed her to the world of architecture weren't some fancy buildings or famous historical figures, but her grandfather who she helped with log cabin building.

*Illustration by Shaikara David*

*"The process of construction and log building and all these other little things that he would get me to do, like stripping the bark, all went into my mind and then led me into getting into woodworking and a drafting program in high school."*

Her high school class led her to wanting to be a carpenter at first, but eventually decided into looking at buildings and *"wanting to go for something bigger."*

But the journey towards her success hasn't always been an easy one. Since around high school, Merasty says she lacked self-confidence, didn't feel like she "belonged anywhere" and "didn't feel confident in being Native."

*"The one thing that really helped me was being around and meeting other people that have experienced the same things that I did."*

Re-connecting with her culture has been a huge help for her as well, and finding those resources in the city has helped her for the past few years. Merasty's mental health is still something she keeps in check and uses health and fitness as something that keeps her grounded.

Today, she would tell her former, insecure self to speak about it [feelings] and not to *"keep everything to yourself."*

*"That's one thing that I used to do all the time. I didn't, I wasn't taught to speak out. I wasn't taught to speak about my feelings,"* says Merasty.

*"I feel like that's something that a lot of our youth should be doing and not keeping to themselves because I feel like that's really harmful in the long run."*

And for students heading into post-secondary, her advice is to utilize every single resource offered.

*"There's so many people that you can connect with that have experienced the same thing that you have."*

*Watch the Future Pathways Fireside Chats video interview with Reanna at https://www.firesidechats.ca/video/reanna-merasty*

# BRIANNA OVERSBY

| | |
|---|---|
| CAREER | Arts / Graphic Arts |
| IDENTITY | Métis |
| PROVINCE/TERRITORY | Quebec |

*Written by Alison Tedford Seaweed*

**Making Art & Community: Brianna Oversby's Journey from Treaty 2 to the Ivy League**

*"Pay attention to the people that are around you and the lessons that they have for you, because there's so much learning that you can do from the people that are around you."* This wise advice comes from Brianna Oversby, an educator and queer person who grew up in Treaty 2 territory (their family are Metis, and German, English & Irish settlers).

Brianna comes by her obsessive desire to create through her family, explaining, *"My dad is such a scavenger and is always like saving trash to turn into something beautiful. Learning that from him has been a huge part of the trajectory in my life."*

*"You can't go far in my house without seeing something that I've made. I'm constantly learning new techniques and skills and building the things around me."*

Creating shaped her career. At the time of filming, she was a program coordinator for the N'we Jinan Integrative Arts Program, where she supported teaching artists as they facilitated creative learning for Indigenous youth from the Harvard Graduate School of Education.

Oversby holds a Bachelor of Fine Arts in Art Education from Concordia university, is certified to teach art in high school and later went onto Harvard University to get her Masters of Education from the Harvard Graduate School of Education.

She also prioritizes informal learning, saying, *"There are a lot of ways to learn outside of school. And if you are interested in learning something with a little bit of effort and asking around you can find the resources to do that. Don't be shy to ask people for help finding stuff because it's available."*

*"Learning new things and making things has always been such a freedom for me. When you learn how to make things, you're able to make any ideas in your head become a reality. That's why art education was so important to me."*

She worked through school crocheting jewellery, working at coffee shops, babysitting, nannying, and briefly as a hotel maid. Later, in New York, she worked for The Leadership Program where she facilitated creative programming for youth after school programs.

*Illustration by Shaikara David*

*"Having the confidence that you have the ability to create the things that you need around you is has had a huge impact on me. Doing things with your hands can be really healing."*

She taught painting, crochet, jewellery making, tinkering, violence prevention and restorative justice programs. Working in schools in New York, she became frustrated with the education system, watching kids who were having difficulty in school getting suspended, expelled and pushed out of the education system there.

*"I couldn't understand why the teachers didn't see that the kids were just kind of needing some more emotional support and needing an outlet to deal with some of the pressures that they were facing."*

That frustration led her to graduate studies where she focused on developing training for teachers to allow them understand kids' behavior and how kids are impacted by trauma and difficult life experiences. Their arts education guided their learning & process.

*"Even in times when I was working in the education system and not necessarily directly connected to art, I was always using creative learning and saw that as a really good vehicle to help people process through the challenges they were facing."*

Oversby's own struggles with anxiety and depression supported her effectiveness in her work. She talks about how arts education guided her recovery.

*"When I decided that it was time to kind of get healthy and take care of myself, I spent a lot of time learning about addiction and anxiety and depression and different ways that I could cope with those things in a healthy way. Creating and making things have always been the major things that I've used to deal to deal with that."*

Brianna has come a long way and flourished in her career. Her advice to youth looking to do the same is, *"Don't sell yourself short. Opportunities that might seem kind of out of your reach probably aren't. As someone who came from a really tiny place and ended up [at Harvard], I never thought that they would let me in in a million years. It became really clear to me that what I had to offer to that community was really unique."*

When it comes to leaving a home community and embarking on an adventure like hers, she recommends staying connected to community and finding community where you are. Looking back, she has a special message for her younger self.

*"You're okay. You're exactly who you're supposed to be. If you've done something bad or something bad has happened to you, those are really important parts of who you are. There's a lot of learning that you can take from those experiencesand they really help to make you more more resilient and more able to deal with situations that life may throw at you. So don't be ashamed of them, embrace them and be proud of where you've been."*

As a maker of art and community, Oversby is inspired by her surroundings. *"I'm really inspired by raw materials. I just love seeing the potential in the stuff that is around me. I think being surrounded by super creative people just has me on fire all the time with like new ideas and new projects. I feel so grateful to get to just spend all the time watching indigenous youth make cool stuff."*

Brianna Oversby is a maker, a creator, a learner and a community leader. She creates and curates, transforms and transcends in a way that inspires. She came from a small community in Treaty 2 and while staying connected to home, she's made a home for herself and others in arts communities.

*Watch the Future Pathways Fireside Chats video interview with Brianna at https://www.firesidechats.ca/video/brianna-oversby*

# NOOKS LINDELL

| | |
|---|---|
| CAREER | Arts / Graphic Arts |
| IDENTITY | Inuit |
| PROVINCE/TERRITORY | Nunavut |

*Written by Jasmine Kabatay*

Nooks Lindell is an Inuk artist from Arviat, Nunavut. As designer for Hinaani Design, he creates both digital graphic art and artisan handicrafts from his home studio. Nooks seeks to create renewed functionality and beauty out of discarded and used items. The reclamation of materials, land, and culture actively decolonizes his artwork and provides pathways to personal healing. Studying the use of objects and the style of Inuit life and culture, he seeks to explore the intersection of the two.

*"When it first started, we weren't really sure if it was going to work or not. It was just kind of a fun project to start, and we started realizing there was a demand and people really wanted clothing that can show off their Inukness,"* said Lindell.

This was started a few years ago and is something they do on the side as they still have full-time jobs.

*"It's a lot of work, but we love it and we know it has a positive impact, so there's a lot of reasons to keep it going and to kind of grow it."*

In the beginning of the business, Lindell says it was "kind of like an art project" and wanted to see if it would work, so three of the designers including Lindell went to an entrepreneurship program with Kivalliq Trade Show, which was a two or three day program.

It helped them out, and they came together with two separate business ideas but after a few days decided their ideas were similar and were all friends who liked working together. So they decided on Hinaani, and the rest is history.

For students thinking about leaving their homes for post-secondary, Lindell says he really encourages it, whether someone is fresh out of high school or even a little older.

He says it's good to get a different perspective on things, and that by leaving your home doesn't mean you don't love it or won't come back to it.

*"Just by going somewhere else, being somewhere else, being with different people, you're going to learn a lot in school, plus just the experience of not being in your hometown, you're going to learn lots,"* said Lindell.

He also says it might even make people appreciate what they have where they're from, and was the case for him when he was living in Ottawa during his youth.

But even Lindell has had to overcome obstacles to get where he is today.

Lindell says shortly after moving to Ottawa when he was eight his father passed away and he used art as a way to help him during that time, drawing for hours and hours getting into his *"own world"* where he didn't have to face reality.

As he got older, Lindell says he moved towards drugs and alcohol to help him escape and created a really unhealthy lifestyle for himself.

With the help of his girlfriend Emma, he quit drinking and started using art as a tool instead of a way to escape.

*Illustration by Shaikara David*

*"When you're addicted to something, in order to stop, it's almost like you need to get addicted to something else. And that's what I did with designing, with drawing, and I also started making jewelry,"* said Lindell.

He says at first he wasn't good at it and almost gave up making his first ulu, but his brother would keep encouraging him and making sure Lindell wasn't deterred. He finished it but wasn't completely happy with it, and made another one asking for the help of family.

*"While I was kind of busy being a drunk, you don't really reach out to family. You don't reach out to your aunts and uncles. You don't talk to them. And so it was so powerful in a way that it was doing something to keep my hands occupied, my mind occupied, but also it was engaging in my culture again."*

And if there is anything he could tell his younger self or other youth, it would be to find someone to talk to about things — whether it's someone in your family, a friend, or even a professional.

Lindell says talking to his uncle who has a lot of similar experiences to him was really helpful for both of them. He also says if going through a hard time to get the emotions out and not be ashamed of them.

*"Letting them build up inside is dangerous and it could really cause a lot of damage mentally, physically. It takes a lot of strength. It's very hard, but I found out talking to my uncles and talking to my family, there's strength in our cultures,"* said Lindell.

*Watch the Future Pathways Fireside Chats video interview with Nooks at https://www.firesidechats.ca/video/nooks-lindell*

# RAVEN BEARDY JENVENNE

| | |
|---|---|
| CAREER | Aviation |
| IDENTITY | First Nations |
| PROVINCE/TERRITORY | Manitoba |

*Written by Jasmine Kabatay*

When Raven Beardy was growing up, she knew she wanted to get her pilot's license — she just didn't know she would make it into a career.

Beardy is originally from Shamattawa in northern Manitoba, but has also lived up in the north in places such as Pond Inlet, Grise Fiord, and Cambridge Bay.

*"Growing up in isolation up in Shamattawa where the only way to get things in and out was by plane,"* said Beardy.

*"So I saw that as a little kid and I actually also got my medevac child as well. I just thought it was really cool, planes were really cool to me."*

Beardy remembers a time when she was seven the power went out in her community and they had to call the medevac to come in.

*"The community got together and actually lined up their snowmobiles along the runways so the plane could land. And I just really thought that was inspiring that the community got together,"* said Beardy.

*Illustration by Kailey Sheppard*

But of course Beardy hasn't always been a pilot. She went to a three-year aviation program in southern Ontario that focused on Indigenous students to become what she is.

Beardy says one of the best things about her program was she wasn't the only one there that wasn't from far away and that everyone was *"in the same boat."*

She says there are many ways to go about getting a pilot's license and people just need to figure out what they want to do.

But of course, becoming the pilot she is today didn't come without its obstacles.

After flight school, Beardy says once someone is finished they usually start working for a flight company and start off on the ground doing jobs such as dispatcher or a customer representative to get a feel of the company.

*"That's usually how it works. And when I graduated with many other pilots, like I was waiting on ground for five years before, or sorry, four years before I actually got a flight position. So it took a long time to get there,"* said Beardy

She said it was discouraging at times and in the end she just powered through it, saying it's very rewarding in the end.

And if there were anything she could tell her younger self, it would be that just because she's Indigenous and a female it doesn't mean there would never be issues.

*"If anything, it was more of an obstacle. I felt like, I had to prove myself even more and work harder than, the next person, which is not a bad thing,"* said Beardy.

*"You're told that you're being Indigenous... [It will be] no problem finding a job or anything like that, but it's not true at all."*

Beardy has achieved a lot of her goals, and says the hardworking people in her life such as her grandparents and seeing their work ethic helped her, along with her parents.

*"I'm very fortunate to have a really great role models in my life."*

*Watch the Future Pathways Fireside Chats video interview with Raven at https://www.firesidechats.ca/video/raven-beardy-jenvenne*

# DANA MARLATT

| | |
|---|---|
| CAREER | Business & Entrepreneurship |
| IDENTITY | First Nations |
| PROVINCE/TERRITORY | Ontario |

*Written by Alison Tedford Seaweed*

*"If I had to sum up my story, it would be one of the spirited and whimsical, gutsy child that lost their spirits and how they found it in the city."* Dana Marlatt, from Port Union, Ontario, the child of a German mother and a Painted Feather Woodland Metis father spoke of their upbringing and how it got them where they are today.

From lemonade stands and babysitting to the restaurant industry and later to academia, Dana's path led to advocacy, personal development, and lessons of following your passions and lateral moves towards fulfilment, but ultimately about balance. Dana burnt out at a startup and took time off to reflect.

*"If you're an innovative person, startups can be a really fun pathway for you, but ultimately I burnt out because I didn't have any support or barriers around that growth. What became really important to me was to think about what my seven year old self would think was cool."*

Dana found joy in work at an animal hospital caring for animals, then paused again to heal from a concussion during the pandemic through offline informal learning opportunities they created for themselves, *"I didn't need to tell anyone or post it on Instagram. It was just for myself and it made all the difference and that's how I found my spirit again."*

A new career evolution would follow at RBC as part of the Indigenous Peoples Development Program, a two-year program rotating work experience in the bank and in charity, providing diversity of thought and horizontal career movement.

*"I've always been involved in a social impact movement. So at RBC that's, #IamRemarkable, which is a workshop that teaches people to speak to their accomplishments and build confidence in the workplace."*

They are also an active member of the Royal Eagles, advocating to promote Two-Eyed Seeing and provide community for Indigenous People at RBC.

Dana learned to be a scrum master, which is like a project manager in tech and is going on to the Canadian Roots Exchange charity as part of their RBC rotation, which focuses on Indigenous research, policy and innovation. The non-linear path of Dana's career brought its own valuable lessons.

*"I've bounced around a lot, but it's really led for such a great cross-cultural exposure from both my own heritage and then the different industries I've worked in and really having that always learning mindset."*

*Illustration by Shaikara David*

Dropping out of high school affected their confidence, creating a sense of powerlessness and a drive to heal from shame through learning. Dana remembers, *"I've really tried to seek out opportunities where I would learn, and it would help get me in a spot where I could then advocate for others."* Hackathons and engineering conferences taught Dana event planning, marketing and other skills.

*"Don't let formal education deter you because sometimes there are socio-economic reasons why you can't attend or maybe like a formal institutional learning environment isn't for you. And that's okay."*

Their advice to youth leaving their home community for university? *"Find mentors, talk to your friends, find communities that have similar values or passions. What I realized is that we're all so connected, especially as Indigenous people or as women or as just plain out human beings, it doesn't matter. There's always going to be a community there for you. You just have to look for it."*

Dana learned something else about the power of community. *"What I really discovered is that their journey doesn't have to feel or be alone. You're allowed to have off moments. And in those moments, I would really call on you to let the people in your life hold up a mirror and show you how strong you are."*

You can get, but you can also give, Dana explains, *"If your bucket's full, you can let a friend take a cup out of that bucket for you and to help remind you how strong you really are. We're all human, we're all going through hard moments. And that's the thing: they are moments. If you can't pull yourself up, ask someone to help you, it's okay to do that."*

*"Just ask. The worst that will happen is someone will say no, and then that's okay, because you can just ask someone else. It's a wild ride to leave home, but it's so exciting. I really just want people to use their passions and what they love and turn it into a purpose whenever they leave home, because that's what makes it fun. Find a community out there that's willing to support you when you're going through hard times because people want to help."*

Dana's mentor Trevor's words also helped, *"Dana, I don't know the last time someone said this to you, but you're whole, and you are worthy."* Those words made a lasting impact, Dana shared, *"I didn't know at the time that it was going to create a really big snowball effect for me, but it did. As a society we're taught to keep attaining and wanting to grow, and you forget that you're already fine as is."*

*"When you're in a crisis moment or a low point, go back to the basics, breathe, drink water, feed yourself, move your body. That doesn't have to be exercise. It can be dancing, it can be singing, but just something to let yourself have a release."*

Dana's crisis management tips reflect Maslow's hierarchy of needs but they also recommend traditional ways of knowing like mindfulness, *"Just focus on the little things and be mindful. Really slow yourself down and it helps... if you're feeling a little bit lacking in inspiration, be mindful, stop and like look at the sunsets at night or go smell a flower, go on a walk and don't take your phone, listened to a new podcast and let yourself close your eyes and just listen. Meditate."*

Dana's big message to the world is one of encouragement. *"I just want everyone to know that they're so accepted as they are and that they're going to find their place in the world. Focus on your mind, your body, your soul, and your purpose and let those guide you and you're set."*

The spirited and whimsical gutsy child that lost their spirits and found it in the city is a true Indigenous mentor and a light for others in their wisdom. Dana Marlatt has so much knowledge to share with the world and so much heart for Indigenous youth.

*Watch the Future Pathways Fireside Chats video interview with Dana at https://www.firesidechats.ca/video/dana-marlatt*

# JESSICA DUMAS

| | |
|---|---|
| CAREER | Business & Entrepreneurship |
| IDENTITY | First Nations |
| PROVINCE/TERRITORY | Manitoba |

*Written by Keith Collier*

Jessica Dumas is a professional life coach who specializes in speaker coaching and business launch for women, she lives in Winnipeg. She has lived in the city her entire life, and growing up in the North End of Winnipeg, Jessica's education and career path is uniquely hers.

*"I graduated high school a little bit late. It wasn't a goal because it wasn't something that my family really had experienced or talked about. I had quit school for a while, had a son, and then I eventually went back to school. It was having my son in my life that really caused me to want to do better. In the last year of school, I had an opportunity to be part of a youth employment program, and right out of high school, I got a job working for Manitoba Hydro."*

*"It was a really good opportunity for a career because no one in my family really worked either and no one had a career, so it was just no big deal. When I started working for Hydro, I was doing customer service and answering calls, I took as much training as I could. I ended up working there for nine years."*

However, a tragedy started Jessica's search for something outside the corporate world. In 2005, her youngest brother was killed by the Winnipeg police, and in the aftermath, she found herself looking for something more meaningful in life.

*"When I left Manitoba Hydro, I started working in restorative justice, and I didn't know what the heck it was, but doing that work allowed me to do a lot of healing and understanding why this happened to my brother. Since making that change from being employed by a crown corporation and the next journey, I started taking a lot of training on my own initiative and continue to do that today.*

Illustration by Shaikara David

*But again, the search for something more meaningful eventually led Jessica to her current work as a life coach and speaker. "I ended up leaving that work (in restorative justice) because I just wanted to see what else is there out there for me in this world? What am I supposed to be doing with my life? What kind of skills do I have? What kind of skills do I want to use? I did a whole bunch of smaller jobs before I got into life coaching."*

Her unique approach to learning and education has served her well, but she admits she struggled with societal expectations of higher education. *"I think our society tells us you have to go to university. And so I really struggled with thinking 'if I don't go to university, I'm not good enough. I'm not smart enough. How do I think I could fit into that next level of your career or profession, and have people look at me in a respectful way?"*

*"I tried university a couple of times and it just wasn't for me. It's not for everybody. I tried to balance it out and say it is okay if I don't have university, I do have a lot of specialized training, and being trained in one specific field, I think is a real benefit to me, but also knowing that it's okay and that it was up to me to accept that. I had a lot of conversations with friends and people who I respected, people who had university degrees and those who don't. And (they) would say things to me like, 'You know your stuff. You don't have to worry about people not respecting you or showing you the credit that you deserve just because you don't have a university degree.'"*

*"I struggled with it for a little while, but then I also realized I met people at conferences or different things, who have degrees in areas that I may have pursued like business or sociology, or things that are kind of an extension of what I do and I realized I was a lot better at my job than they were, and so I thought, 'You know what? I don't need a university degree. It's not for me, and that's okay!' I have a lot of training that I've taken, like life coaching certification training, facilitation training, advanced business design facilitation. I used to be a little bit insecure about no degree, but not anymore."*

As she transitioned from her corporate career into coaching and speaking, Jessica also struggled with various challenges, including finances, networking, and balancing her responsibilities as a mother. *"A lot of my career journey had to do with what was going on in my life. As an adult, I lost my brother. I became divorced and had to raise three kids as a single parent. There were a lot of shifting priorities between what I want to do for my kids and how I wanted to provide for them, and I recognized that in order to give them a life that I want, I need to do something that I really enjoy so I would be happy."*

Throughout her varied career, Jessica has learned that self-confidence is key to success. *"When I was leaving a permanent job and talking to people about starting a business and being a life coach, people would tell me that I was crazy. People told me I should just go back and get a job. I should always have a job because I need to feed my kids. And so I really had to build a lot of belief in myself because I wasn't finding it anywhere else, because I had this strong desire in me to just keep going and doing it."*

*"I always say you have to believe in yourself. That's part of the challenge of wanting to do something totally different because not everybody's going to say, 'Oh, that's a great idea. We'll help you.' And sometimes that's really hard to hear, especially if you have kids and you're raising your kids because that alone is a huge responsibility."*

True to her work as a life coach Jessica offered listeners seven pieces of advice:

1. Learn your history, because until you know who you are, you're still going to be searching.

2. Learn your gifts. We're all born with natural skills and gifts, and our gifts are meant to give away.

3. Learn where you belong, because we all belong somewhere. We go through times where we feel like we don't belong anywhere, so it's important to learn where it is that you belong.

4. Don't be afraid to ask questions. Ask questions whenever you can and never feel stupid about asking a question because you're expanding your mind.

5. Think beyond the limits that you know. When she was young, no one she knew personally had a career. No one she knew graduated high school, owned a car or a business. But when she had her son, she started to imagine bigger and that really allowed her to open up her life to bigger things.

6. Have fun with life. Jessica really believes that life should be fun, and that doesn't mean being careless, that doesn't mean just not giving a crap about anything. Have fun, but in a respectful way.

7. And love. When we talk about it, we talk about it so sarcastically, but love is a really amazing thing.

*Watch the Future Pathways Fireside Chats video interview with Jessica at https://www.firesidechats.ca/video/jessica-dumas*

# DIANE ROUSSIN

| | |
|---|---|
| CAREER | Community Development |
| IDENTITY | First Nations |
| PROVINCE/TERRITORY | Manitoba |

*Written by Oscar Baker III*

**Diane Roussin said keep moving forward because eventually you'll get where you need to be.**

Diane Roussin remembers a time when she felt completely out of place. She moved to Winnipeg from Skownan First Nation to attend university but she didn't even know what a major was. And as a Anishnaabe woman in mainstream society she felt less than those around her. But she pressed forward and after two degrees and a wealth of knowledge from other Indigenous women she's the project director at The Winnipeg Boldness Project.

And she wants to Indigenous youth to keep pressing forward.

*"You will figure out what's right for you. You will figure out where you need to be. So just keep going. But you don't have to know all that ahead of time and no one can tell it to you anyways,"* said Roussin.

She knows firsthand when you come from homes with family violence or alcoholism one can find themselves questioning why they are there or feeling like second class citizens. But Roussin says it makes more sense when one learns about colonialism and that many poor conditions are forced upon Indigenous communities.

And to this day those conditions still make angry but she credits her heroes and other Indigenous women for helping her to be vulnerable and offering her support.

*Illustration by Shaikara David*

*"They love and hug and dry your tears and just surround you with all that caring and love Indigenous women just do so much for me. That is my go to, and that's how I get through a lot of tough stuff,"* said Roussin.

And from their advice she has three pieces of advice; 1) Keep a support system. 2) Lay down tobacco, remember Indigenous culture is important and 3) Keep things relative, things may be hard but there are those in the world suffering more.

Roussin says she went into social work because she always wanted to help people and after a practicum she knew she wanted to help integrate the field with Indigenous ways of knowing and caring.

*"I feel like Indigenous knowledge systems totally know how to deal with all of what's going on right now and totally know how to get through tough situations,"* said Roussin.

*Watch the Future Pathways Fireside Chats video interview with Diane at https://www.firesidechats.ca/video/diane-roussin*

# JENNA WIRCH

| | |
|---|---|
| CAREER | Community Development |
| IDENTITY | First Nations |
| PROVINCE/TERRITORY | Manitoba |

*Written by Alison Tedford Seaweed*

From surviving to thriving: Jenna Wirch Creates Opportunity for Indigenous Youth

*"I grew up in Winnipeg. I grew up in poverty. I grew upon the streets, homeless, in CFS care. I didn't want to stay in the same cycle as my peers and as my family."* Those are the words that Jenna Wirch, The One Who Sings With The Grandmothers, uses to share her story of how she went from surviving to thriving and how she helps others do the same.

A member of Bear Clan and of Long Plain First Nation, Wirch started a group called AYO, Aboriginal Youth Opportunities, with a colleague. As the name suggests, for ten years, they've been providing Indigenous youth with opportunities to better themselves.

*We're trying to break stereotypes in our neighborhood by being helpers, and not being those stereotypes that society places on us as Indigenous youth.*

She talks about her work as *"fixing the systems that are in place that oppress Indigenous young people, helping out family, just being a true helper and doing the work that needs to be done without being asked to do it and not asking the government for help."*

An influx in gang activity in the north end of Winnipeg left Wirch and her cofounder wanting a positive outlook for Indigenous young people to go to instead of having to join a gang.

*"What do gangs bring to the table when Indigenous young people need an outlet? When there is nothing around they provide family, they provide safety, they provide job opportunities, but that just wasn't sufficing for us."*

Wirch wanted to offer something different, explaining, *"What we have now done is become a positive gang. We provide hope, meaning, purpose, and belonging. That's essentially what our four pillars of our work that we do."*

After grade 12, Wirch went through post-secondary education through an access program. To become a registered child care practitioner, Wirch reached out to community resources.

*"I didn't want to continue the cycle of poverty. I wanted a good life for myself and my community around me."*

She hasn't stopped learning. Wirch shares, *"I'm unlearning all the unhealthiness that I've learned throughout living in poverty and living on the streets and living a hard life, and healthy coping mechanisms, my past trauma, learning how to heal myself."* She found community for herself and wants youth looking for something more to find it too.

*"If you're coming to a big city that is unfamiliar to you, remember that you are loved, that there are people out there and just look for your community and look for your village. You need to create that sense of belonging and recreate that community that you once had, because that's how you're going to get through in this life. You are not alone.*

*There will always be a community that you belong to. When you move to a big city, in every single city, there is a friendship center. There is a place that feels like family, where there is people who are inclusive and won't judge you. You just gotta keep at it and believe that you can make it because you can."*

Her words for her younger self are similarly infused with compassion.

*Illustration by Shaikara David*

*"Just chill, everything happens for a reason. you can get through this. You're surviving and you will make it through. Keep going. Reach out to your community and don't be afraid. Don't be afraid because we're all in this together. We've all had to do it.*

*I know it's hard, but like other people who have been through it, we're out here and just reach out, because we know what it's like. We have a lot of opportunities to provide to help and a community that you belong to."*

Wirch has faced a lot of challenges from the outside and even some from within, like panic attacks. Through meditation and medicines the elders have taught her, she finds comfort.

Whenever I'm going through a panic attack, I remember to breathe and I light a smudge and I pray and I ask the ancestors to be with me.

A drummer and I'm a singer, Wirch pulls out her drum and sets energy out into the world. *"Creator gifts me back with the patience. At times of uncertainty I just prayed to creator to like ask him that he take care of me and I put all my faith in what is to come."* She also makes lists of what she can and can't control and all the things she's grateful for.

Wirch is inspired by the speed of learning of the young people of today, by their courage and how they have been resilient despite genocide against Indigenous people. She's inspired by the Indigenous community as a whole and to the elders that keep and pass on the teachings, hoping to become one of those old *"kokoms"* one day.

We have been going for 500 years and we are still thriving. We count as 5% of Canada, we are still out here strong, and we haven't left. They tried to kill us, but we are still here.

Looking to the old ones and the strength of community, Wirch wants to pass that onto the young people of today. She says, *"When you're moving on from your community, from that old lifestyle, I want you to know that you are loved. You is kind, you is smart and you is important and reach out to your elders and reach out to other youth around you, because you matter, and don't give up. We need you for the next seven generations to come."*

She herself went from surviving to thriving, from living on the streets to building community and from needing a chance to creating opportunities. Forward-looking, with respect for the past, breaking cycles and showing up to serve, Jenna Wirch is making a difference.

*Watch the Future Pathways Fireside Chats video interview with Jenna at https://www.firesidechats.ca/video/jenna-wirch*

# ASHLEE FOUREYES

| | |
|---|---|
| CAREER | Computer Science |
| IDENTITY | First Nations |
| PROVINCE/TERRITORY | Alberta |

*Written by Alison Tedford Seaweed*

Ashlee Foureyes is from the Maskwacis, Wetaskiwin area in Alberta and is a software development engineer with Amazon. After growing up in a rural community with limited access to technology, Ashlee started her education with the idea that her love of math would translate well to accounting which she was studying at the University of Northern BC. She soon found out that was not her path and decided to take a coding elective.

She fell in love with computer sciences and moved across the country to study at Carleton University. Ashlee went to a small high school with people she had been going to school with her whole life so university was an adjustment. She found UNBC to be a good stepping stone between high school and a big university like Carleton. While she might have been intimidated, she made sure to be social.

*"I just forced myself to get out there and step outside of my comfort zone."*

Ashlee's advice for college students is *"seek out people, join clubs, make friends."* While at UNBC, Ashlee really enjoyed the community of a smaller school and she wanted to avoid being in a big city lecture hall. She enjoyed the Indigenous resource centre and found it helped her feel connected to the community.

Smaller colleges with university transfer programs can be an option to ease the transition, Ashlee suggests. Something she discovered she really loved when she got to Carleton was hackathons, which aren't what you might expect.

*"You think it would involve a lot of hacking, but it doesn't."*

*"A hackathon is basically a mini conference where you get together with a team of people and you create an app,"* Ashlee clarified. Hackathons allowed her to compete, learn and have fun while travelling within her province but eventually as far away as Helsinki. Hackathons are one way to get exposed to solving real world problems in a way that mirrors the workplace.

*"When people think about computer science, they think you're going to be a programmer. That's not always the case. There are different career paths that you can take."*

The reality is the possibilities are endless. Whether you're lit up by the creativity of UX design, the math of machine learning or software engineering, or the business side of Product management or consulting, Ashlee explains how there are so many choices.

It isn't just different roles, with a variety of industries hiring people with technical backgrounds, passion can meet purpose in choosing a career. Even without childhood coding experience, technology is an option for youth later in life.

*"It's really just like learning a language. Once you start immersing yourself... you'll see it become easier as time goes on and it's just that initial hurdle that you need to get over."*

While many of her peers had been coding since they were young, Ashlee started in college. She initially felt at a disadvantage and like there was a learning curve, but she found her pace and resources to help her catch up. That learning prepared her for the career of her dreams.

Ashlee met Amazon at Grace Hopper, a software engineering conference for women. Now her days start with standup meetings and transition to independent project based work and team meetings. Ashlee's first job after university was with a small tech company in Calgary, but she found her way to Amazon soon after. She brought her adaptability with her to shine in her new role.

*"Being able to adapt to evolving situations is a skill that I think has been transferred over throughout generations."*

Looking back at her resourceful and innovative ancestors and considering her culture, Ashlee sees how the adaptability she was raised with has made her ideal for working in tech. Programs like Amazon Future Engineer brings computer science education to remote communities, giving unprecedented exposure to technology and opening doors for Indigenous youth like Ashlee. With the right opportunities in reach, Ashlee encourages young people to dream big.

*"Never sell yourself short. Just really believe in yourself and find what you're passionate about and be confident that you can achieve your goals."*

While internet connection can be a challenge, those technical skills can be assets to a young person's home community. Recent events have shown you don't have to be in an urban centre to work in tech, you can work remotely too. The pandemic that put the spotlight on remote work has created mental health challenges, and Ashlee shared her advice on getting through tough times.

*"Get outside as much as you can and get into a routine I guess. And just keep in mind that better times are coming soon. Just focus on the positive."*

Just like she looks to solve problems in her work with Amazon, Ashlee found ways to get by during the isolation of the pandemic. Connecting through technology like Zoom and FaceTime, getting fresh air and exercise were other tips that Ashlee had for overcoming the pandemic blues.

An inspiration for her insights for pandemic coping and for the way she has pursued her passion for computer science into a dream job, Ashlee is lighting the way for Indigenous youth everywhere. Her pioneering spirit, creativity and problem solving skills, passed down to her through generations of her family, truly make her a role model and an asset to her community.

*TakingITGlobal is pleased to have Ashlee's involvement as a First Nations role model and guest speaker in the Connected North program. Amazon is also supporting coding and computer science education learning opportunities for Connected North's network of schools through the Amazon Future Engineer Canada initiative.*

*Watch the Future Pathways Fireside Chats video interview with Ashlee at https://www.firesidechats.ca/video/ashlee-foureyes*

# DALLAS STORM FLETT-WAPASH

| | |
|---|---|
| CAREER | Computer Science |
| IDENTITY | First Nations |
| PROVINCE/TERRITORY | Manitoba |

*Written by Jasmine Kabatay, Illustration by Shaikara David*

Dallas Flett-Wapash is new to what he does but is already full of promising ideas. Flett-Wapash, from Keeseekoose First Nation but currently lives in Brandon, MB, works as a game designer as well as an interactive artist.

*"It's very fulfilling. And so if you're passionate about video games, then that makes that time just pass by a lot faster. It doesn't feel like work. And it's really fun,"* said Flett-Wapash.

Flett-Wapash was motivated to make video games when he was a kid, because they would make him feel emotions. As he got older he noticed the lack of Indigenous video games in mainstream or Indigenous characters in a *"self-determined way."*

*"Part of my ambition is to fill some of that gap myself, but also to aid others in believing they can do the same,"* said Flett-Wapash.

When he was 10, he had the ambition to make games but not the know how, and says his training was informal and self-driven.

He spent a lot of time after school with a camera shooting video in his home and would edit the video on his computer, learning the process by using Google and finding free software he could use for his craft.

When he was in grade 12, outreach programs from various cities came to Norway House where he was at the time and noticed Assiniboine College in Brandon.

They were advertising a program that would teach students about graphic design and web design. Flett-Wapash wasn't passionate about web design, but figured there were other things he could still learn within the program.

*"While I was studying there, I was able to delve into game design in these self-driven projects, which I'm ultimately super grateful for, because they could have just stuck to the status quo,"* said Flett-Wapash.

After studying there, he went to Brandon University to study fine arts and strengthened his design skills alongside his development abilities.

He is currently working on a game where the player plays as a piece of bannock on a *"cartoony adventure"* with a sidekick and through the process of the game the user would also learn an Indigenous language.

It's something he's still working on, and will continue to do so for the next year or two depending on funding and other things. He hopes to release it on something more accessible to Indigenous people.

*"I don't want to necessarily divide people by what console they have, but something that I do see that a lot of Indigenous children have is a lot of them have these phones to play games on or iPads to watch YouTube videos on and stuff,"* said Flett-Wapash.

For students leaving their community, he says there will be a mix of pain and freedom given to you, but there are ways to alleviate the pain and managing the freedom.

He lived with his family in Norway House Cree Nation, but moved away from his family to study in Brandon. A lot of Flett-Wapash's pain came from not hearing his mother or brother talk as much as he was used to hearing them in his house. The sudden change made a bit of a difference and says the silence was *"seizing"* and made him not want to do things.

*"I think a proactive approach would be putting yourself out there and maybe finding people who are in similar situations that you both can come out stronger from it,"* said Flett-Wapash.

He also thinks one of the most powerful things one can do when leaving their community is to consider what the goal is for leaving, whether it be to go and come back with a skillset the community needs or even just to have a voice heard.

*"I think just internalizing that and understanding what it is it can be a good motivation for when you get down, when you're outside of your community."*

The biggest obstacle he faced was learning to become independent and learning to live without his family by his side. It was personable for him because he spent a lot of time with his family, and even more so before he moved away from the community.

He navigated that by finding like-minded friends and playing games with them, and scheduled calls with his family so he would still be talking to them on a regular basis.

And if there were one thing he could tell his younger self, it would be there is always a solution to a problem.

*"You need to find the best way to identify that problem, verbalize it. And don't be afraid to seek help and finding the solution to that problem."*

*Watch the Future Pathways Fireside Chats video interview with Dallas at www.firesidechats.ca/video/dallas-storm-flett-wapash*

# CARLY CHARTIER

| | |
|---|---|
| CAREER | Culture |
| IDENTITY | Métis |
| PROVINCE/TERRITORY | Manitoba |

*Written by Jessica Dee Humphreys*

Carly's path has certainly been closely tied to her Friendship Centre, one of over a hundred across the country. As a teen she took on a volunteer position, and then worked with the youth programme while she was in college, before moving into the administrative position she holds today.

The Selkirk Friendship Centre is a large operation with programmes running in several different locations throughout the city. Carly explains, *"We have a childcare programme, we have an apartment building; our youth programme building is the next street over which houses afterschool club, youth mentorship, and the HeadStart programme, which is a preschool that's Indigenous-based."*

Carly's work at the Centre is constantly evolving. *"When I started working there, we were more into like the developmental stages. So we did a lot of employment. Getting youth inspired to go back to school, to get their Grade 12, to move into college, getting those programmes to help them find employment and stuff like that. And then really focusing on mental health and physical health."*

Carly was first inspired to take on this kind of social work through a sociology class in high school. *"That kind of stuck with me and I really liked it. I really liked my teacher and we connected."* In college, Carly found her specialty after researching some of the classes that were being offered in human behaviour. She selected them purely out of interest, only to learn that they could lead her to a career. *"I didn't even know it was a part of a whole certificate of Human Resources. So when I went to sign up for the classes, [the college advisors said], 'Well, maybe you'd be interested in these ones, and then you could actually graduate.'"*

Illustration by Shaikara David

Not surprisingly, then, Carly's advice to youth would be to do their research as they plan for their future. *"All of the colleges and schools actually have people that are available to talk to about things. So if there's anything you're unsure of, just ask."*

Carly had watched too many friends jump straight into college from high school without taking the time or making the effort to research what might actually interest them. *"They did a year of it, and that's not even remotely close to what they actually finished in. And I just felt like that's so much time and effort and money that you're putting into it that's not benefiting you and going anywhere."*

Being wise about savings is the one piece of advice Carly wished she could go back and give her younger self. *"Thinking back to when I was 16 to 21, the amount of money I spent on stupid things that looking back now, I was like, 'That's so much money I could have put towards something else and saved up.'"*

Much like researching courses at school, Carly advises seeking out the experts when it comes to financial literacy. *"You could call up your local bank and speak to a financial advisor. Most of them won't even charge [youth]."*

And when the time comes to seek employment, *"I really encourage people to research other jobs than the ones that are forward. When you go to a job fair, yeah there's all those set jobs, but there's also so many behind the scenes that you don't see."*

Carly wants young people, especially Indigenous youth, to *"know your worth!"* She wants them to do the research and understand the wages they are entitled to. *"I know a lot of youth get taken advantage of and right away they're thrown the minimum wage. But a lot of times, if you have that one or two years experience, you're entitled to a bit more of a pay raise. Do not be afraid to ask for one if you deserve it... Always research what you're doing."*

*Watch the Future Pathways Fireside Chats video interview with Carly at https://www.firesidechats.ca/video/carly-chartier*

# CURTIS CLEAR SKY

| | |
|---|---|
| CAREER | Culture |
| IDENTITY | First Nations |
| PROVINCE/TERRITORY | British Columbia |

*Written by Oscar Baker III*

Curtis Clear Sky says Landback for Indigenous people means food security because food is grown by the land.

Curtis Clear Sky remembers the first time he accepted the offer to go out to the UBC farm, and the mix of people who boarded the bus. As they drove past the trees, Clear Sky was amazed at all the growing things and believed they had like 20 acres of farm. But the real joy began when they sat down for a community dinner - Clear Sky realized food was medicine.

*"For me, I knew at that point, I felt like, man, this feels really right. This feels good. I wanted that to happen again. I thought to myself, I got to make this happen again. I got to make sure that I'm getting involved and I'm supporting the community and getting involved in creating spaces like that, where we can sit together, enjoy food together, and that we're no different from each other. That we're all the same. We're all one. We're connected,"* said Clear Sky.

And he's been working for food security ever since. From 2013-2016 he was working with the Tyu'wut Project at the UBC farm and now works with the First Nations Food System Project which helps over 70 First Nations communities in British Columbia gain autonomy over their food.

And for Clear Sky food security means getting the land back.

*"So there are systemic social impacts that have caused harm for our people and that connection to food and the urbanization of Indigenous peoples,"* said Clear Sky, and he

added some people have chosen to move to urban centres to seek opportunities but colonization has disrupted Indigenous connections to the land. *"We need to reclaim our connection to our territories."*

Clear Sky is Blackfoot and Anishinaabe says his people have always had a deep connection to the land and the food they ate and harvested. And says the land loss Indigenous communities have suffered have led to food insecurity. But through acts of resistance people like him are trying to reclaim those connections to food.

*"Building those relationships and those strengths are one of the keys to empowering ourselves. The knowledge is something that we still can attain. Our connection is something that we can reclaim. It's a beautiful thing when we're able to reconnect and reclaim those things,"* said Clear Sky.

Clear Sky is also a musician with Curtis Clear Sky and the Constellationz and as he moves as an artist he believes food and music often intertwine. And in the meantime Clear Sky will continue to advocate for food and how special it is to Indigenous people.

*Illustration by Shaikara David*

*"One of the first things that I've learned in my experience in relation to food is that food is a spiritual experience. And for us as Indigenous people, food has always been a spiritual experience for us. It's what has sustained us, it's what's given us our lives,"* said Clear Sky.

Carly Chartier works with the Selkirk Friendship Centre, as well as being a hobby photographer and artisan specializing in moccasin-making. She is Métis, raised in Selkirk, MB and her family is from Sagkeeng First Nation, in Treaty 1 territory.

Carly's association with the Friendship Centre started when she was just four years old; and her family would attend the various programmes held there. *"We did powwow dancing, there were culture nights, gym nights, all that stuff."* While she imagined it must be an amazing place to work, it never occurred to young Carly that she would end up there as an adult. *"It's really neat to kind of loop back. Some of the co-workers I work with actually were the ones that worked there 20 years ago when I used to come as a small kid."*

This is a key element of these important Indigenous community hubs: *"A part of the Friendship Centre is just having those relationships and showing how much they actually connect people for a lifelong journey."*

*Watch the Future Pathways Fireside Chats video interview with Curtis at https://www.firesidechats.ca/video/curtis-clear-sky*

# JOY HALL

| | |
|---|---|
| CAREER | Culture |
| IDENTITY | First Nations |
| PROVINCE/TERRITORY | British Columbia |

*Written by Jasmine Kabatay*

Joy Hall says her love for farming started when she was learning about traditional medicines — now it's her career. Hall is an organic vegetable farmer and owns a quarter acre vegetable farm on Skowkale in the Stolo Nation Territory, and is actually on her family land behind her house.

She started becoming interested in farming when she was working in a workshop with the chief and other leadership, and they were talking about departments they were going to take over and start running on their own.

Hall says someone mentioned agriculture and growing their own food, and it sparked her interest. She went on to research what kind of schooling she would need for that, and applied for the agriculture program at UVF.

*"When I was supposed to register for the program, I got an email saying that my funding fell through. I wasn't able to register for school that year. I was very disappointed about that,"* said Hall.

She was scrolling through Facebook and an ad popped up for Tsawwassen farm school through Kwantlen Polytechnic University.

*"I clicked on that and everything just sort of fell into place,"* said Hall.

She didn't have funding, so she contacted the farm school coordinator who suggested she contact the Sto:lo Nation and she went for it.

*Illustration by Shaikara David*

*"I called, went to an interview, they told me the next week that they were going to pay for school. I went and applied for it, got accepted,"* said Hall.

She also went to her work supervisor and asked if she could move to part-time due to her new venture. Her supervisor originally denied her, until Hall said she was going to have to leave her job and was then approved.

Hall then started school at Tsawwassen farm school where she was commuting back and forth to from Chilliwack, which she says is about a 45-minute drive but on bad days could take an hour and a half to two hours.

Farm school is only one season, and after that Hall had a knee surgery so she wasn't able to farm. But the institute for sustainable foods systems at Kwantlen contacted her and asked if she could work on a project with them.

They named the project the Sto:lo Nation Farm to Healthy Communities project, where they recruited community members that have diseases related to food like diabetes, obesity, heart problems, etc., to give them free organic vegetable boxes every week.

They wanted to see if access to those organic vegetables would help them with their health problems, and Hall came on as a liaison to help with it.

They also wanted her to be the farmer, but she had to have a year of farming under her belt on her own. So she had to get out there right after knee surgery.

*"With the help of my sister, my mom and my nephew we got out there and we just started farming, started making the beds and planting everything. That was the first year that I farmed,"* said Hall.

The next year, she started a CSA box program (community supported agriculture), which had 10 boxes the first year, and quickly grew to 40 in the next couple years.

*"This is my third year. The project went really well. It helped a lot of people with their issues like weight loss and stuff like that, with their health and food security, giving them access to the organic vegetables,"* said Hall.

And for anybody thinking of following a similar career path as her, she says to just do it.

*"I think everybody should be growing their own food, it's fun when you're out there, you feel grounded. It connects you back to the land."*

*Watch the Future Pathways Fireside Chats video interview with Joy at https://www.firesidechats.ca/video/joy-hall*

# TAYLAR BELANGER

| | |
|---|---|
| CAREER | Culture |
| IDENTITY | First Nations, Cree-Métis |
| PROVINCE/TERRITORY | Saskatchewan |

*Written by Alison Tedford Seaweed*

**Growing Where You're Planted: Taylar Belanger's Healing Journey**

*"I've actually always been super connected with mother earth at a very young age to the point where I'd eats soil and dirt and I'd also actually go out and find earthworms and keep them as pets,"* Taylar Belanger explained.

A meeting with another matriarch about five or six years ago helped her gauge her path. Belanger got very sick two years ago and needed to find an alternative bay to help herself heal outside of Western medicine.

*"I've just been very connected with plants my whole life to the point where I would feel and touch them and just feel a very strong connection with them."*

Elders and healers told her, *"You actually are supposed to be working with traditional medicine. So learn as much as you can and keep going down that path."* She found Wild Rose College that offers herbalism certificates and diplomas.

Currently in a three-year practical herbalism program, a further three-year clinical herbalism is next. She's learning plant identification, herbology, the science behind plants, their medicinal properties, and how to identify them. She wants to use that information to help people in need with an alternative way for healing.

Her advice about leaving your home community for learning opportunities like she did is simple, *"Never forget where you come from, because those are where your roots are. Always bring something back to the community so that you can show what you've learned and so that we can be better as a community as well."*

*Illustration by Shaikara David*

From a young age, she has been aware of energy and emotions and the powers they carry and how they influence people in their day to day lives. Because of this, she has found herself being comfortable spending time alone and managing how she responds to energies that surround her.

*"Music has always just been my go-to low key and I'm finally coming out with it."*

As a youth, music was important to her and she would later bring that back into her world in her artistry through the work she does under her artist name, Soca. The notes and frequency of music were calming to her.

*"[Music] allows me to express in a way I would never be able to express with words. It also allows me to be creative."*

One of her most recent musical expressions is a music video called Protector, which she considered a positive song. *"That's essentially my call-out for us coming together as people and our men also coming in and being the protector that they're meant to be. I think we're all healing and we're all in this process,"* she explains.

As another creative outlet, Taylar is a self-taught traditional tattoo artist. A lot of her inspiration comes from petroglyph on rocks that carried Indigenous people's stories.

Her advice to youth is around being true to oneself. *"Just stick to what you love, find out what you love to do and learn to master it. A lot of the time it's very common where we're forced to do something that is not really meant for our spirit and meant for us. But if we always do something that makes us happy, then we're going to be happy for the rest of our lives."*

Music, reading and picking medicine help Belanger manage her mental health. *"Because I'm in the city right now, I can't really actually go out and pick medicine, but I'm going back home and picking medicine is something that makes me feel good. When you pick, you also have to think of good thoughts,"* she shared, explaining how she catches her bad thoughts and turn them into a positive

When it comes to inspiration, Belanger looks within to inspire herself, but she's also inspired by people around her. *"When I see other people just being strong and resilient and just having that strength and people who have integrity, who are honest, who are super respectful and humble, that really inspires me because that allows me to be who I am without being judged or without people being a certain way. I would say integrity inspires me a lot. Passion inspires me a lot. Just seeing people happy, inspires me a lot."*

As she works to study plants to help her community heal, Taylar Belanger is growing where she's planted, leaning into the roots she's put down and reaching upwards towards the light. A source of positivity and calm, Belanger is grounded in who she is and what she offers the world.

*May 2023 updates: Taylar has been keeping busy! Taylar is in the final year of her practical herbalist diploma, onto clinical herbalism. She is looking forward to expanding into Naturopathic Medicine to become a licensed Naturopathic Doctor and serve her community and the far North in a natural and holistic way. She is currently the program coordinator for The Kiya Land Based Healing Project for her community of Sakitawak. Furthermore, she is also a coordinator for a Northern Indigenous Women's Network working with a project called Raising Their Voices. They advocate for Indigenous women and the LGBTQI2S+ community finding their voices and stepping into leadership roles. She is also working with elders to develop a plan to build a ceremonial healing lodge in her community.*

*Watch the Future Pathways Fireside Chats video interview with Taylar at https://www.firesidechats.ca/video/taylar-belanger*

# HANWAKAN BLAIKIE WHITECLOUD

| | |
|---|---|
| CAREER | Entertainment |
| IDENTITY | First Nations |
| PROVINCE/TERRITORY | Manitoba |

*Written by Jessica Dee Humphreys*

Hanwakan Blaikie Whitecloud is a filmmaker (and passionate skateboarder) from the Sioux Valley Dakota Nation. His latest documentary, Star People, examines Indigenous views on the stellar origins of human beings. Whitecloud explains: *"a lot of the makeup of stars, like iron or carbon and different atoms and molecules that are in the stars, are in us. So in that sense we are stars, right? And we come from a mother star, which is the Earth."*

Such beautiful and dynamic imagery speaks to Whitecloud's seemingly limitless energy and creativity. But it wasn't always easy for him to explore that side of himself. Whitecloud's early years were burdened by expectations of conformity to a system that *"looked down upon Indigenous people."*

*"We're finally getting to a place where we're staring to not be like that, but"* he recalls, *"when I was growing up it was not a good thing to be Indigenous."*

Despite his parents being fiercely proud Indigenous people and trying to instill that pride in him, Whitecloud felt that actually worked against him at his mostly-non-Indigenous school. *"I always had super Native t-shirts on and that probably wasn't a good idea at the time. My dad was always like, 'Just be proud.' But it really put a target on my back, and I got bullied quite a bit."*

Feeling he didn't belong or fit in made for lonely school years for Whitecloud, who also struggled with the formal, academic side of school all through elementary and high school. Despite poor grades and active discouragement from teachers, guidance councillors, even the employer at his part-time job, Whitecloud was determined to go to university.

*"The people who hired me kept putting me on full-time shifts. And I was like, 'I need to go part-time because I've got to graduate high school.' and they were like 'No, you should work full time,' and they just kept scheduling me. I was like, 'No, no, I got to graduate,' and they were like, 'Nah, don't worry about that.' And I was like, 'That's it, I quit!' Because I'm going to graduate high school and I'm going to go to University. And it just felt like they didn't believe in me."*

Whitecloud explains that what he was experiencing was systemic racism: *"They looked at me like I was an 'other', like I didn't belong and so they didn't believe I could fully integrate with the system, that I could be successful."*

This attitude, which Whitecloud faced throughout his young life, informed his poor self-esteem. *"If people don't think that you're ever going to be successful, you in turn start believing that you're never going to be successful, and so then you have to battle that. And battling that is a really tough one because sometimes you believe you're not worthy of things like scholarships or opportunities."*

*Illustration by Shaikara David*

Without many role models, Whitecloud tirelessly pushed to fit in to the system that surrounded him. He persevered through school, working part-time jobs until midnight each night before a short sleep and returning to classes in the mornings. He worked in call centres (where he learned valuable interviewing skills), he delivered mail for Canada Post (where he learned that keeping moving and interacting with people were how he thrived), and he worked his way through the Winnipeg Public Library system. It was there that he was convinced that sticking with *"the system"* and following the rules would guarantee his employment and success.

However, *"when I graduated University, I applied for over a hundred jobs and I only got called back for two, one for a sewer maintenance worker and something else like a clerk. And I was totally destroyed initially because I was like, 'Whoa, I did everything right.' I went to school, I went to University, and I haven't got in trouble with the law. I've been a good person, but I was never rewarded properly. Or at least I felt like I wasn't."*

Whitecloud was shocked to discover that his attempts to fit in had failed him. But as an adult, he recognizes some key realities: *"In this current moment when I look back on my life, I'm like, oh, that totally makes sense, because we still have a lot of systemic racism."* Also, it wasn't until he was an adult that Whitecloud was finally diagnosed as having ADHD (a diagnosis which, if it had come earlier, would have likely improved his academic experience exponentially). And, he received counseling to address his feelings of low self-esteem.

*"I started going to counseling right around the time I was diagnosed with ADHD, and talking out self-doubt questions in my head with somebody who I felt safe to do so with really helped."*

*"[My councellor] has been able to frame my life and how I've been behaving in certain situations that's normal. It's totally normal and it's like those situations were not right, and people weren't treating me right. It wasn't about me being bad....I actually was a positive person. I just wasn't perceived well in certain situations."*

With the insights afforded by both his counseling and his diagnosis, Whitecloud is able to forge his own path, instead of trying to accommodate the status quo. As an example, he now recognizes *"the education system doesn't really support youth in the way it should. We shouldn't be sitting at desks all day."*

Once he was released from his mental shackles, Whitecloud found his path. *"Being physically active is huge. That's why skateboarding is so huge to me, because it was always being outside, and always meeting different people, and also having fun!"*

*"I had a boss [who told me], 'If you're having fun, I don't think you are doing your job.' And I started to think about that. I was like, 'Is that true?' But the more you talk to other people, the more it's like, no, no, no, that's wrong. That's not right, that's unhealthy. That is a really unhealthy way to look at life."*

Finding the *"fun"* in life and in work was actually what motivated Whitecloud to enter filmmaking. *"Every project is fun. Because travelling with people is fun, meeting new people is fun, and just trying to get different angles and create a story, all that I found very fun."*

Skateboarding was Whitecloud's original *"focus for fun"* where he discovered filming while skating to find those perfect shots. *"We started using video cameras and photos, and from there I just kept doing that and eventually it was 'Oh, I want to make professional stuff.'"*

Since making these discoveries, Hanwakan Blaikie Whitecloud has travelled from New York to Nunavut to Newfoundland filming his documentaries, skateboarding as he goes. His overcoming obstacles to discover his true worth and view the world through his own unique lens (both figurative and literal) is an inspiration to us all.

*Watch the Future Pathways Fireside Chats video interview with Hanwakan at https://www.firesidechats.ca/video/hanwakan-blaikie-whitecloud*

# MICHELLE CHUBB

| | |
|---|---|
| CAREER | Entertainment |
| IDENTITY | First Nations |
| PROVINCE/TERRITORY | Manitoba |

*Written by Alison Tedford Seaweed*

Many people know Michelle Chubb from TikTok, but she's really from Winnipeg. A celebrated Indigenous TikTok personality, Chubb is from Winnipeg Bunibonibee Cree Nation (Oxford House), an isolated community ten hours from Winninpeg.

Chubb's mother is from Cross Lake but she herself grew up in Winnipeg, in St. Norbert, in the south end. She found the transition from Rez life to City life tough, noticing how people looked at her differently because she looks different. After graduation and a lifetime of isolation, Michelle found she bloomed socially. She was looking for community but got lost along the way.

*"I was just trying to find my character and what to do. I fell into drugs and alcohol. I fell into the wrong crowd. I lost myself and I found myself again by reconnecting with the culture and I am a year sober from alcohol and drugs."*

As she got sober, Chubb learned, *"You've got to figure out your own things on your own, what you want to do in your life, because it's your life and your story."* She shares her story on TikTok with her audience, but it's not a platform she always took seriously.

She watched TikTok videos on Youtube with her boyfriend and found them entertaining. Later, she decided she wanted to try something new. After her attempts to go to university at U of M for engineering didn't work out, she was eager for change.

A few months after starting her TikTok, it was a success. She started getting more gaining more and more followers each day. People were now following her, but she was thinking about who she followed as a younger person to find her own way.

Chubb was introduced to ceremony and powows by her grandparents. Her grandfather later passed away and then her mother shared culture with her too. Wanting to finish her Sundance years, Chubb's mom brought her along. Her family connected her with culture and it's helped her on her way to TikTok stardom and in navigating everyday life, making mistakes but finding her way back.

She took a gap year after she tried out university, moving to Cross Lake to live with her grandmother. Unfortunately, she fell in with the wrong crowd and found her life was spiraling. While at times she struggled with finding positive connections in *"the real world"*, she's carved out a place for herself where she can share her culture online.

She struggled through the ins and outs of the technical end of TikTok, and she's glad she did. She had a vision for her online presence that was around giving back.

*"I wanted to help out my younger self, if that makes sense. I wanted to help others because I had trouble when I was younger. I want to be there for those youth also who are having trouble and are lost."*

She records messages for her audience all the time, but she has a message to students leaving home community so they don't feel so alone and overwhelmed by the culture shock of coming to a big city:

*"My old friends had trouble adapting to the City life. They had trouble with loneliness. You've just got to stick through it. Not everything is going to stay the same. You've got to embrace the difference and just stick with it, persevere through the hard challenges and you'll get there."*

City life has created challenges Chubb has had to overcome. *"I experienced a lot of racism, obviously. In City life, you can see it, but you just choose not to do anything about it because you're scared for yourself. Racism is a big factor, especially with the Rez life too, and not being too Rez or not growing up in the Rez, you're looked at differently."*

Between racism and lateral violence, Chubb has navigated struggles in the world at large. She faces problems on TikTok too. She shares about those, saying, *"There will be a lot of comments, just stupid questions or plain racism and a bunch of ignorance, but I just choose to ignore it because not everyone will have an open mind, not everyone is willing to accept what you say. So you can only just grasp the eyes that you can catch."*

Looking back, she wishes she could say to her younger self not to take life too serious, not to overthink things and to accept that not everyone is going to like you. She's come a long way, but like anyone, she has to work to keep her mental health in check during challenging times.

*Illustration by Shaikara David*

*"I keep myself busy. You've got to keep your mind busy. You can't just keep thinking about bad thoughts. You've got to get rid of that negative energy. I've been going back to working out again."*

While she's inspired by the past and culture of her community, Michelle Chubb is focussed on building in a way that's forward-looking. She says, *"I want to see a better future for the native community and myself and just a better future in general."*

In a digital world that can sometimes feel manufactured and contrived, her message is one that values authenticity, sharing *"I would like to say to everyone to stay true to themselves."*

Michelle Chubb is an inspiring young woman focused on unapologetically being herself, staying sober and connected to culture, and being part of a healthy community in a viral world. While her success is reflected in followers, it's really reflected in the strength of her community and her confidence in sharing who she is with a world that didn't always understand her. Like the content she creates, Michelle Chubb's journey is a story worth sharing.

*Watch the Future Pathways Fireside Chats video interview with Michelle at https://www.firesidechats.ca/video/michelle-chubb*

# RICHARD PELLISSIER-LUSH

| | |
|---|---|
| CAREER | Entertainment |
| IDENTITY | Mi'kmaq First Nation |
| PROVINCE/TERRITORY | Epekwitk - Prince Edward Island |

*Written by Jasmine Kabatay*

When it comes to physical training, Richard Pellissier-Lush might be the one to help out. Pellissier-Lush (Kitpu Amalkewinu - Eagle Dancer) is from Lennox Island First Nation and grew up for the majority of his life in Charlottetown, PE, but was originally born in Winnipeg, MB. He has done a lot of things regarding health and fitness since his time playing football in high school.

After college, he went on to do multiple jobs, like becoming a personal trainer, working for the Jordan's Principle program, working with the Aboriginal Sports Circle, and PEI Aboriginal Sports Circle.

But it wasn't always that way. Pellissier-Lush says when he was a kid he was chubby and absolutely hated sports, saying every sport he tried he ended up quitting.

It was when he was in grade 10 and could have strayed either between a life of athletics or a life of crime and gangs, which some of his friends at the time were headed.

But before that could happen, football tryouts were starting up.

*"I had a couple of friends that were on the football team. They encouraged me to be on the team. I gave it a shot and I absolutely loved it,"* said Pellissier-Lush.

*"It kind of created this passion for me and this passion that really strayed me to the opposite side that I wanted to be. So I was no longer even thinking about that gang of violence, that crime side."*

*Illustration by Shaikara David*

After playing a season in Manitoba, he moved back to Prince Edward Island with his family and joined the football team at his school there for the next few years where he became all star every single year for the PEI Tackle Football League.

Shortly after, he started thinking of a game plan to play for the Manitoba Bisons because of his past knowledge of the team and he knew the coach.

*"I just kind of shot out the dark. And I sent him an email and said, 'Coach Doby, I'm really interested in coming to play for the Manitoba Bisons, what do you think the chances are?' And he shot right away, almost instantly back,"* said Pellissier-Lush.

The coach told him they would love for him to try out and thought he would be a good fit for the team, so Pellissier-Lush went to Winnipeg, tried out, and made the cut.

But the transition for him wasn't an easy one. He says he got into the party scene a little bit and that the academic transition was something that was difficult for him as well.

*"The education kind of came front first at me. And I wasn't doing as well as I expected. So the first year, I got through it, but I wasn't doing the best that I could have been,"* said Pellissier-Lush.

He says at the time there were a lot of distractions, including friends with different life paths and priorities than him and that he didn't know what his priorities were for himself — he just knew he wanted to play football.

After his stint at the University of Manitoba, Pellissier-Lush decided it was more of a better fit for him to go to college. So he went to Holland College in PEI who at the time was creating a brand new football program.

Though it was an easy transition for him, Pellissier-Lush says if he were to tell himself something today it would be to utilize all the resources that the University of Manitoba had to offer him.

*"It was just because I was too proud of myself. I was too proud and I didn't think I needed the tutoring. I didn't think I needed the mentoring, but those resources were there,"* said Pellissier-Lush.

*"If you need help in something, ask for it. People are always willing to be there and support you whenever you can."*

*Watch the Future Pathways Fireside Chats video interview with Richard at https://www.firesidechats.ca/video/richard-pellissier-lush*

# MUMILAAQ QAQQAQ

| | |
|---|---|
| CAREER | Government |
| IDENTITY | Inuit |
| PROVINCE/TERRITORY | Ontario |

*Written by Jessica Dee Humphreys*

Mumilaaq Qaqqaq is an exceptional young Indigenous leader and advocate for Inuit. She was the elected Member of Parliament for Nunavut from 2019 to 2021. Born in Baker Lake, she now lives in Iqaluit. Mumilaaq was elected in 2019, when she was only 25 years old. Prior to that, she rose to acclaim in 2017 when she gave a powerful and emotional speech about the Indigenous suicide crisis, as a representative of Daughters of the Vote in the House of Commons.

Mumilaaq's path to the halls of power was not straight, and it took her all the way across the country. After finishing high school, she started programmes at three different colleges; first, in Charlottetown, Prince Edward Island, then in Peterborough, Ontario, and finally at Algonquin in Ottawa. However, she never completed any of these degrees. *"So technically, I just have my grade 12!"*

*"I took sport and leisure management, and now I'm a Member of Parliament. I don't know how much farther away you can get,"* she laughs. These educational stops and starts helped Mumilaaq keep an open mind when considering her future. *"You might not pick the career you end up with. And that's fine. That's perfectly fine. I'm 26, I'm an MP, and I still don't know what I want to do with my life. Career choices can change. You might think you're interested in something, and maybe you find that you're not totally."*

Mumilaaq wants youth, and even adults, to know they have the power to make a change in their lives. *"We put way too much pressure on our youth, and on younger adults, to figure things out so quickly. It's fine if you don't. Perfectly fine. I still haven't, and I think I'm doing pretty okay."*

Despite her outward confidence and strength, Mumilaaq still has moments of doubt. *"There are hard days where I don't know if I'm doing the right thing,"* she admits. "*Quite often in our lives we are our biggest barrier, our biggest, worst critic."* Though Mumilaaq is often lauded for being an inspirational role model, she sometimes struggles against her inner voice. *"I go and work 14 hours in a day and I still don't feel like I'm doing enough."* She has to remind herself of her strengths, and speak kindly to herself. *"[I have] this weird inner dialogue that says, 'No, you belong here, and you're meant to be here.'"*

When she sits in the House of Commons, Mumilaaq is too often confronted with 'not belonging.' *"I get stopped by security when I'm on Parliament Hill,"* she says. *"I'm not a bald white man, so I get stopped a lot. I definitely have really hard days where it's like, maybe I'm not supposed to be here. Maybe I'm not supposed to be a part of whatever the system."*

*Illustration by Kailey Sheppard*

Of course, Mumilaaq knows this is not the case; she not only belongs, people like her are essential to bettering our system of government.

*"So many of these systems in place are not built for Indigenous people, are not built for racialized individuals, are not built for women. So I spend a lot of my time [reminding myself], 'I belong here. I belong here. I belong here'. I know my truth. I know my history. I know the truths and history for my constituents."*

Mumilaaq has always had a strong voice, making her an excellent advocate for Inuit. *"I think that as Inuit, we've done our time of taking a back seat and listening; it's time for us to have a voice in things that directly impact us... It is time that we see more voices that look and speak like mine, especially at those huge decision-making tables."*

However, if she had one piece of advice for her younger self, Mumilaaq would suggest listening more, speaking less. *"Sometimes when I look back, I wish I could just close my own mouth and sit myself down, and say, 'Just soak it in and listen.' I think we all go through that. It's confusing growing up."*

As a child, Mumilaaq always wanted to be older and make her own decisions. *"Now I'm an adult, and I'm like, 'Where's my mom? I want my parents! Someone make decisions for me, please!' But that's not how it works."*

Mumilaaq treasures the love, guidance, and support her parents provided her. *"They've moved mountains for me and my brother. I feel really lucky."* And she advises young people who have a supportive family to *"really enjoy the time that you have with your family... I wish I really invested more energy and positivity into those relations when I was at that age, but we're working on it now. Life is all about learning."*

As an advocate and as a politician, Mumilaaq is paving the way for Indigenous youth to be heard. *"The thing that for years and continues to frustrate me is that in society and in the 'adult world' or whatever you want to call it, is that we don't involve youth as much as we should, as much as we could. [Young people] want responsibility. We want to be included. We want to contribute and be part of our future. And we have every right to do so."*

*"I think it is more than okay to push for a seat at the table. It's more than okay to speak up. And the worst thing that we can do for ourselves is choose silence over choosing opportunities that allow us as individuals, us as families, us as community members to have that potential option to actually be a part of the decision making, to influence what the future is going to look like for us."*

*"Because it's our future. We're going to be here much longer than a lot of other people. And I think we're starting to see a movement where we're seeing youth that are much more realistic, analytical, have better and greener and more inclusive solutions. And that we're starting to see a shift in mindset about who can do certain jobs and who can't. And I would just say if you want to be there and if you want a spot at the table, go for it, fight for it! And if that's truly what you want, don't let anyone tell you you can't."*

*Watch the Future Pathways Fireside Chats video interview with Mumilaaq at https://www.firesidechats.ca/video/mumilaaq-qaqqaq-mp*

# SENATOR YVONNE BOYER

| | |
|---|---|
| CAREER | Government |
| IDENTITY | Métis |
| PROVINCE/TERRITORY | Ontario |

*Written by Jessica Dee Humphreys*

Senator Yvonne Boyer has had many careers — first as a nurse, then as a lawyer, and finally as a Senator — which have all melded together to inform her life's work to improve the wellbeing of Indigenous people. Referring to herself as Michif, Senator Boyer is Métis, with Chippewa, Cree, and Irish ancestors. She was born and raised in Saskatchewan, and currently resides near beautiful Merrickville, near Ottawa.

*"I have the most beautiful grandfather teepee in my yard... I lay tobacco down every day and I go talk to the trees. And through these last months [during Covid], we haven't been able to go anywhere, but I certainly found my solace with Mother Earth here. I have three really favourite trees and three favourite grandfather rocks that are out in our meadows, our sacred meadows. So it's nature, it's nature that has really grounded me here. I've been isolating with my grandchildren who are seven and five. And we do teepee teachings in the teepee every Sunday and we talk about stories that I was told as a child."*

Senator Boyer has always been very connected to her family. *"My dad was the youngest of 14 children, so I had many, many aunts and uncles. He was very, very loved, so I came from that aspect, that the aunties and uncles loved him and they loved me. That's how I was raised."*

Especially influential for Senator Boyer were the stories told to her by her Aunt Lucy, who contracted tuberculosis when she was 14 and spent a full decade alone in the Fort San Sanatorium in Fort Qu'Appelle. *"She only saw her family once in those ten years. And back in those days, they didn't have antibiotics, so they treated it with sunshine and rest. They said, 'Rest is the cure.' And 'rest' meant no movement whatsoever. That meant lying on your back, not moving. [...] Five of those years, she was in a complete body cast."*

*Illustration by Shaikara David*

This vivid image was just one that deeply moved Senator Boyer. Even more galling were Lucy's stories of cruelty and injustice that the Indigenous residents of the Sanatorium faced. *"She told me about how it wasn't always fair and how sometimes monsters walk the halls. And sometimes things happen to children that really was not nice. She talked to me about the difference between the kids that had family close by and the kids that didn't have any family close by, and the kids that were Indigenous and the kids that were not Indigenous and how they were treated. She talked about the experiments that were done, and she talked about death and dying and coughing and coughing and coughing and people dying and friends dying and what it was like to be flat on your back and at the hands of the people who were supposed to be taking care of you."*

Senator Boyer comes from a family of healers, and she was expected to follow that path. So after graduating high school she went into nursing. Working at small hospitals in central Alberta, Aunt Lucy's stories came to life for Senator Boyer. *"I saw what she had been talking about. It was 30 years later and it was the same thing and there were the same monsters walking the halls at that time as well. [I got] angrier and angrier and angrier about what I would see, and how Indigenous people were being treated, and some of the comments that people made to me (because they thought I was like them) such as, 'Those Indian women need to be sterilized so they don't reproduce.' That was something that I heard on more than one occasion. And the more I heard it, the more I got angry. And I came to a point in my life where I was driven, like there was no alternative. I was absolutely driven to do something about it."*

While working full time and raising her young children as a single mom, Senator Boyer started *"picking away"* at various night classes. *"I wasn't sure what kind of tools I needed to get. I didn't know if I should go into social work. Would I be effective? Would people listen to me then if I was a social worker? Would I have any control over what I was seeing in the healthcare system? And then it just sort of came into my lap."* Senator Boyer found herself enrolled in a class in Human Justice. Her professor, who was also a practicing lawyer, was so impressed with a paper she wrote for the class, he told her, *"'I would offer you a scholarship if you went to law school.' And I said, 'What? Really? The law?' And he started talking to me about the tools that you can get in the law. And so it was at that point I was convinced that somebody actually believed in me. He planted a seed in my head."*

She never did take him up on the scholarship, but she acknowledges: *"He gave me a much bigger gift of being able to envision what I could do."*

In 1991, Senator Boyer and her children moved from Nova Scotia, where they had been living, all the way to Saskatoon so she could take the Legal Studies for Native People summer programme. *"I had three children under eight, two suitcases, a borrowed car, and no job."* And as soon as she arrived to launch her law career, she realized she had something else as well. She was pregnant.

*"I didn't know what to do. I was full of complete self doubt. Can I do this? And at this point, it probably became one of the most powerful lessons I ever had in my life. I'm in tears, I'm at the beautiful campus at U of S, and the summer program is starting. I see a woman and she's one of the profs teaching in the summer program. She's got long hair and she's got a long skirt and she's got a bunch of kids with her and she's pushing a baby carriage and people are following her, talking to her. And I thought, 'Hmm, I think I should talk to her.'"*

That woman was Trish Montour. *"She is a force beyond belief. She has now gone to the spirit world, but she made an impact in everybody's life that she came across."* Senator Boyer sat down with Professor Montour and poured out all her worries. *"I'm crying, crying, saying, 'I don't think I can do this. Oh, no, no. I got all these kids. I got no job. I got no money. I got nowhere to live.' And Trish, in her matter of fact way, she put her arms on her hips and she said, 'Of course you can do it! Are you crazy? You've got the gift of being able to go home and chill out with a brand new baby on your breast. And you can study the law on one hand and you've got these gifts that nobody else will have. And you are above that. You can do this there's no doubt about it.'*

*"And that was a turning point in my life where once I believed I could do it and I had — once again — somebody saying, 'You can do this.' And I did." I made it through the program, and I made it through law school, doing the best she could. I didn't get the top grades, but I didn't fail anything, "and nobody's ever asked me about my marks, ever."*

Through those rough years, without scholarships or other financial support, Senator Boyer succeeded in working, raising her kids, and getting her degree, and yet still didn't have a lot of confidence. In her cap and gown, on the stage, waiting for her convocation, she caught sight of the Dean of Law and was afraid he would tell her she hadn't actually qualified. *"So I beat it across the stage and took my degree and ran like hell. And I said, 'I will never go back into another university,' which was really funny because as Indigenous people, somehow you don't think that you are actually deserving of this. You didn't quite do it well enough or something, and that's not at all true. I want to dispel that myth right off the top!"*

Now sitting in the Canadian Senate, Senator Boyer has both the confidence and the authority to advocate for Indigenous people in powerful, meaningful ways. Her main area of interest is equitable healthcare for Indigenous people. *"As a legislator, I have an incredible opportunity to make change. And I would like to see all of Canada's legislation [reviewed] to ensure that it is equitable for Indigenous people." Of special note in her work is Section 35 of the Canadian Constitution which states: "The existing aboriginal and treaty rights of the aboriginal people of Canada are hereby recognized and affirmed."*

Senator Boyer wants all Indigenous people in this country to understand Section 35. *"There are no laws that are more powerful than that. ...We have Aboriginal and treaty rights that are protected by the constitution. So I look at it from the perspective that I have an obligation. I've done quite a bit of work on ancestral medicine, or ways of being, and I put that into an Aboriginal Rights perspective under the protection of the constitution."*

Similarly, the Senator is careful to remind us of inherent Indigenous laws: *"Our ancestral laws are as powerful, if not more powerful, than the Western law of the Constitution. So those two are the bodies of law that I work with. And I take them both very, very seriously."*

In regards to these laws, Senator Boyer is passionately involved in the areas of justice and consent around the abhorrent sterilization of Indigenous women and girls. *"I've stayed up nights thinking about how do we fix this one. Because the problems are so inherently ingrained."* The Senator is looking carefully and thoroughly at the issue from many angles, to find a solution that works within the existing structures of both federal and provincial jurisdiction to end this heinous practice.

This is how the Senator works tirelessly, every day. *"I get legislation, I look at it and the first thing that comes to mind is, 'How is this going to affect Indigenous people in Canada? Does it touch on their rights?' And because of my legal background, I have the ability to look at legislation and be able to do that. And that's the gift I have of getting those law degrees that allow me to do that. And it's a responsibility that I take very seriously."*

Senator Boyer is one of 10 Indigenous Senators (*"strong, powerful people in the Senate that are held up by their ancestors"*), and she wants to encourage young Indigenous people to learn about the Senate. *"We need you to get your education so that you can join us, because you're the next generation that's going to take our places. You're the next generation of leaders and role models.*

*"And I'll tell you, thinking about where I came from, the last thing on my mind when I was growing up is that I'm going to be sitting in the Senate. That never crossed my mind. Nor did it ever cross my mind that I was ever going to be a lawyer. But take advantage of what you're seeing and listen to your heart. I know now that none of what I do is a 'job'. This is a calling. I was called here. I was called to do this. So you'll know that. You follow your heart and that's the way you're going to be able to make change, because you now have to think about who's going to take my place. I'm only there for another few years, and then we need you to come up and take our places. So I'm looking forward to seeing that. It's a good succession plan."*

And her advice, to young people with questions about what they should be doing: *"It's a big, great adventure out there. Trust your instincts. If you have a question about what you're doing, or if you've got something that you're worried about, or there's a big decision to make, write it out on a piece of paper, put it under your pillow, and ask the ancestors and say a prayer. When you wake up in the morning, you're going to have those answers. It might take a couple of nights, but help is available. Just put it out in the world, put it out in the universe, and the answer will come. Just ask, that's all. People and our ancestors are there to help you."*

*Watch the Future Pathways Fireside Chats video interview with Senator Yvonne Boyer at https://www.firesidechats.ca/video/senator-yvonne-boyer*

# PIHÊSIW CRANE

| | |
|---|---|
| CAREER | Health & Science |
| IDENTITY | First Nations |
| PROVINCE/TERRITORY | Alberta |

*Written by Jasmine Kabatay*

Pihêsiw Crane shines as a complete force in their line of work and says it was something that just *"fell in their lap."*

From Maskwacis-Samson Cree Nation in Alberta, but currently lives in Edmonton, Crane is a queer, disabled, full spectrum Indigenous birth worker and sexual reproductive health educator.

They do support in everything, from support in miscarriage, support in abortion, support in adoption, fostering, surrogacy, and also works with LGBTQ+ youth and other vulnerable youth.

They also teach sexual reproductive health through the Native Youth Sexual Health Network and works with a group called Indigenous Birth of Alberta whose whole focus is providing culturally appropriate care to Indigenous families while also incorporating traditional birthing practices with Western medicine.

*"I've been volunteering with families, birthing people and babies since I was about 11. I used to volunteer at Red Deer Regional Hospital and I worked in pediatrics, maternity and NICU,"* said Crane.

*Illustration by Shaikara David*

But it was when they were pregnant as a teenager that their work really started. Crane was 18 weeks when they lost their son and didn't have any supports from within their community and within the hospital, which caused a lot of trauma.

Then one of their friends was telling them about how they worked as a doula and Crane thought it "sounded weird" until they were told what it was and found it was something they were doing for a while without even knowing.

*"So I took the training on a whim. I contacted a trainer within Edmonton and it was just like, "Hey, can I do this? I have no idea what this is about. Let me do it."* And she's like, *"Okay."* Paid the money and did the training and absolutely fell in love with the work," said Crane.

A year later, someone found them on Facebook and asked if they were interested in being part of an organization to provide support to Indigenous families and they agreed, which was the start of Indigenous Birth of Alberta.

Their full spectrum job began when Indigenous Birth of Alberta and NYSHN were emailing back and forth and decided to do a worker training for it, with Crane at the time both training other birth workers and also learning through NHYSN.

*"Before NYSHN, I didn't do any full spectrum. I did just births and I didn't even know 'full spectrum' was a thing. And NYSHN came and it was really nice to be able to do training with other Indigenous people and to be trained by Indigenous people,"* said Crane.

When Crane thinks back to the loss of their child and how it started the work they're doing now, that it was healing for themself and for other people, and says they're always learning something new.

Crane's education about their career is huge and constantly evolving, but growing as a foster child in the system being bumped around made it difficult to properly receive a western education.

They didn't receive their grade 12, but is currently working on it right now going to NorQuest College and upgrading on their courses. In the fall time they will be going to the University of Alberta for native studies.

*"Which I am terrified because it's been seven, wait, 2014 is when I graduated. So it's been not seven, six years since I've been out of school. And I'm just very nervous,"* said Crane.

But Crane has been through an incredible amount of obstacles in their life, from growing up in the child welfare system to health conditions, they've stayed resilient through it all — and credits the community for it all.

*"I think really what gave me the strength to persevere and continue on and reach my goals was my community. Even though I was very detached, I always knew that they were there,"* said Crane.

It's also something she would tell youth who are thinking about leaving their community for the first time.

*"Regardless if you didn't grow up in your community or if you're leaving your community, they're always there and the one thing that I love about our Indigenous communities is they're always so welcoming."*

*Watch the Future Pathways Fireside Chats video interview with Pihêsiw at https://www.firesidechats.ca/video/pihesiw-crane*

# JAMES HARPER

| | |
|---|---|
| CAREER | Skilled Trades |
| IDENTITY | First Nations |
| PROVINCE/TERRITORY | Manitoba |

*Written by Alison Tedford Seaweed*

**Culture of Sustainability: James Harper's Perspecive on Renewable Energy & Indigeneity**

*"This vision of always considering seven generations is so moving to me because it's the true definition of sustainability."* James Harper is a Cree man making waves in renewable energy, inspired by his ancestors and thinking of the youth of tomorrow.

James Harper's Cree name, Mihskakwan, means *"red cloud"*, and was gifted to him by his mom who raised him with his two sisters. She graduated from law school while raising her kids, instilling in them strength, discipline and inspiration.

Like his mom, Harper pursued post-secondary education, completing a Bachelor Of Science In Mechanical Engineering at the University of Manitoba in 2017. He's currently working on a Masters degree in renewable energy. In studying sustainability, he's been able to travel to places like Stockholm, Barcelona, and Paris. His vision is one of integrating renewable energy and clean tech into our energy systems of tomorrow.

Harper is a proud citizen of Sturgeon Lake Cree Nation on Treaty 8 territory; he was born in Edmonton and grew up in Winnipeg, which he now calls home. *"My whole experience as a Cree man has been mostly pretty much urban. I don't necessarily have the experience of growing up within a community or learning so much about the traditional relationship with the land,"* he explained. Despite being urban-raised, he notes that he maintains a strong relationship with his family, especially his kookum or grandmother, who has gifted him many teachings on what it means to be Niheyaw (Cree).

While navigating the challenges of intergenerational colonization, Harper looks to empower Indigenous communities across Canada. So far, that's looked like SevenGen, the First Indigenous Student Energy Summit which he developed and organized to include over 300 Canadian students.

*Illustration by Shaikara David*

*"We wanted to bring awareness into the ability for youth to understand their inner strength and empower them to believe that you can make a difference even in your own communities and even at a much bigger scale. And all it takes is one person."*

The conference included energy speakers, Indigenous leaders, clean tech experts, and entrepreneurs, all with a goal to share the urgency, importance and goals of renewable energy and how it impacts global climate.

For Harper, what he does has been intrinsically tied to who he is as an Indigenous person and his family values. That's the perspective he brought to SevenGen participants and that he brings to work every day.

*"I understood more about my fundamental roots as a Cree man and where I come from and understanding what my ancestors wanted me or envisioned their children to be doing and as a reflection too, of what they strived very hard to do as well, which was to protect our earth for the children of tomorrow."*

Striving towards the targets laid out in the Paris agreement make sense to Harper, he explains, *"I grew up with these Cree principles of caring for the land and loving our children, those unborn generations ahead tied in with the current climate crisis that we're in with all these initiatives, all these reports and all these findings that urge everybody to act now."*

While formally educated, Harper values informal education, mentorship and relationships with established leaders and elders. He draws wisdom from formal and informal education, but also from the land, saying, *"As much as I can, I will get myself out onto the land because it is the best classroom. It is the best teacher."*

He's had many opportunities to learn, but Harper still struggles against imposter syndrome, feeling like he doesn't fit in and isn't smart enough. He tries to focus on what he brings to the table, explaining, *"The world would be a much better place if everybody was there and present and had their voices heard."*

When he thinks about youth leaving home to start their own journeys, he wants them to hear this advice, *"Just breathe, just relax. It is very overwhelming and it's totally okay to feel overwhelmed and anxious. It's totally okay to reach out to your support system."* He also encourages youth to stay present in the moment and connected to each other.

Harper's grandmother taught him, *"As long as you're somewhere on this earth, you are connected to all of us." For Harper, that's translated to more than just relationships to people but also to the earth, "No matter where you are, you're connected to the land."*

His own advice to youth is to take risks and stop worrying about failure, leaving behind the *"what if"*'s. He says, *"In the end, it's not a failure at all. It's just another stepping stone for you to grow into a well-rounded human being."*

He's no stranger to risk and the innovation it can bring. He helped build an experimental vehicle to compete against other teams, placing 17th out of 22. While they didn't win, him and his team gained an unforgettable experience, lasting relationships, and important skills that would be very important in his career.

To keep his mental health on track, Harper challenges himself creatively, meditates, stays active, engages in continual self-directed learning, connecting with people and finding joy, all with a goal to spiritual, emotional, physical, and mental balance.

While focussed on the future of renewable energy, Harper is inspired by the past. He thinks about the adversity and sacrifice of his ancestors, pushes forward to honour them by excelling in his field and pursuing his dreams.

Through the life he builds researching and developing renewable energy, Harper wants a lifestyle where he can not only have fun but also preserve the joy of future generations by protecting the earth.

Ultimately, Harper encourages people to be proud of where they come from, and he reflected on his own journey in that respect. *"It took going really, really far away to realize what's really important, which is where I come from and home and my family that brought me there in the first place."*

James Harper's work deals with the the renewable energy of science but in reaching out and connecting across Canada, he's also leveraging the renewable energy of Indigenous youth. The passion and awareness that comes from those interactions bring another kind of power that gives hope for the future and for Indigenous people everywhere. Staying Healthy In A Viral World: Michelle Chubb on Indigenizing TikTok.

*Watch the Future Pathways Fireside Chats video interview with James at https://www.firesidechats.ca/video/james-harper*

# KRISTA PAUL

| | |
|---|---|
| CAREER | Skilled Trades |
| IDENTITY | Métis |
| PROVINCE/TERRITORY | Saskatchewan |

*Written by Jasmine Kabatay*

Krista Paul has a love for helping people both inside and out, and found it in the beauty industry. Born and raised in Saskatoon, Saskatchewan, she is a hairstylist and makeup artist and has been in the industry since 2009, changing and evolving throughout it all.

Paul went to cosmetology school for 10 months, where she learned things that she both expected and didn't expect.

*"One of the things that I didn't really think of was the physiology of the body and understanding it and knowing it. So that was probably the hardest time in school,"* said Paul.

A lot of the focus was on hair but she also learned about makeup and *"the basics of everything,"* but in doing so "you don't really get to know a whole lot."

So for the first five years of her career, Paul didn't take any extra education and worked at a salon to try and figure out what was next for her. Eventually, after staying at the same salon for a few years, Paul was questioning her career.

*"I started to question whether or not I should still be doing hair because I just didn't have the spark anymore. I kind of felt like I kept doing the same thing over and over and over,"* said Paul.

She moved on to another salon and was introduced to more education about hair, taking a class about colour and learning more about it and *"going back to the basics and fundamentals."*

*Illustration by Kailey Sheppard*

*"That's when I was like, 'Oh, this is amazing,' because it just like reinvigorated my passion and it re-inspired me. So ever since then, I take so many education classes throughout the year."*

Growing up Paul had no idea what she wanted to do or even if she wanted to be a hairstylist, she just remembers being young and cutting her friends bangs or styling their hair.

*"I always had this little knack that I didn't think was part of my talent or you know what I naturally do,"* said Paul.

She also says people have assumptions about hairstyling saying it's fun she gets to *"play with hair all day,"* but it's so much more than hair for her.

*"One thing I always go back to is, I love helping people, but I get to help people on the outside and then on the inside,"* said Paul.

*"That's why I became a hair stylist is because connecting with people and just making people feel their best."*

Getting to where she is now wasn't easy. Paul says one of the things she had to face that was difficult was starting out and trying to figure out who exactly she was, because it's *"what's going to drive you."*

Another obstacle she faced was not being in the right environment where she could thrive.

*"Sometimes you outgrow your environment depending on who you are because you change constantly,"* said Paul.

*"Don't ever stay somewhere that doesn't make you feel good, or even in any other industry or career path you choose. If you don't feel good in that environment, find another environment that you can thrive because sometimes you outgrow it and sometimes you can keep growing."*

*Watch the Future Pathways Fireside Chats video interview with Krista at https://www.firesidechats.ca/video/krista-paul*

# SATEANA GOUPIL

| | |
|---|---|
| CAREER | Skilled Trades |
| IDENTITY | Inuit |
| PROVINCE/TERRITORY | Nunavut |

*Written by Jasmine Kabatay.*

Sateana Goupil has always been fascinated with electricity, so when he had the opportunity to become an electrician he took it.

Goupil is from Iqaluit, NU, and has lived in various places in Canada and the U.S., such as Quebec, Ontario, Kansas, Connecticut, and more.

Goupil works as an electrician, and says he had always been fascinated with electricity since it is used in everyday life. He became interested in the trade when he was living in Wichita, Kansas, where his partner at the time had a family friend that worked at a construction electrical company.

Knowing he wanted to get into the trade, he used his family and friends network and was able to start an electrical apprenticeship.

*"When I was presented with the opportunity, I started off as green as you could be. And they had me digging trenches. And eventually helping out setting up the circuitry, inside three separate buildings,"* said Goupil.

*"At that construction site, I was able to learn how to do an equivalent of residential applications, and commercial, and industrial electrical wiring."*

But before he became an electrician, Goupil played junior hockey in Ottawa when a former coach offered an opportunity for him where he was able to go for a 10 game try-out in Danbury, Connecticut.

*Illustration by Shaikara David*

Through networking, he was able to meet Todd Stirling, who ran a master's hockey school and through communicating with him, he was able to head to Connecticut.

*"After the 10 game trial, I had outplayed the other rookies on the team, and they decided to keep me for the remainder of the year. And through the travels in the US, I was able to also go to Bloomington, Illinois, Wichita, Kansas, Laredo, Texas, and Alexandra Bay, New York,"* said Goupil.

He says those experiences helped him learn not only about himself but also about the different types of cultures within one country.

*"I'm grateful for those opportunities. And I feel that recently, having received my Journeyman electrical ticket, I've been able to reflect and appreciate the experiences a little more,"* said Goupil.

Even though Goupil has had an interesting journey, it's one that has also been met with obstacles.

For Goupil, one of the major obstacles was moving away from his father and stepmother's home. He says he found that challenging at first, because it was hard to find a new normal in a setting he wasn't familiar with.

He says that while being in Connecticut enabled him to be away from home, it was also a seven-hour drive for his father to come see him, which helped ease the anxiousness he was feeling.

Goupil also says when playing hockey, growing up he was used to playing people within a three to four year age gap but was all of a sudden playing against men with that were sometimes 10–12 years older than him.

*"You realize that these, your new peers at that point are more mature. They're stronger. They're mentally fit. And they're capable of staying consistent,"* said Goupil.

*"I found that was one of the things that was the most challenging. Trying to be consistent while learning to be comfortable away from everything that I was used to."*

Goupil is still involved in hockey and coaches children. He feels he was very fortunate to be given opportunities to play on high-level teams and learn from excellent coaches during his career, so he felt it was important to give back.

*"It's fulfilling to be able to see some of the traits you're wishing to pass on to those you're coaching. I feel that sport is so powerful. And it enables the youth to hone in on some life skills that they'll use later on,"* said Goupil.

*"You're trying to teach concepts and systems, but ultimately, you're preparing the youth for their future jobs, and trying to teach them some of the values that you were taught growing up."*

And for people thinking of leaving their community for post-secondary or a career, Goupil encourages anyone to chase their dreams.

*"Be passionate about what you choose to do. If it is a path through college or university, recognize that your family will be there. Many of the things that you enjoy doing at home, cherish those moments when you have an opportunity to go."*

*Watch the Future Pathways Fireside Chats video interview with Sateana at https://www.firesidechats.ca/video/sateana-goupil*

# CARSON ROCHE

| | |
|---|---|
| CAREER | Sports and Recreation |
| IDENTITY | First Nations |
| PROVINCE/TERRITORY | Northwest Territories |

*Written by Alison Tedford Seaweed*

**Playing For Keeps: Carson Roache's Connections Through Sport**

While Carson Roache teaches play and games, he takes the work he does as the program coordinator at the Aboriginal Sports Circle of the Northwest Territories seriously. His enthusiasm is contagious. *"I've been here for just over two years and I don't plan on leaving. I love my job and it's going awesome so far,"* he shared with excitement.

Originally from a small town, Délı̨nę, which was called Fort Franklin in Northwest Territories. An hour and a half flight from the capitol city, t's a town of 400 people. Isolated, remote and primarily populated by Indigenous people, Roache left in grade eight to get a better education. Now, he lives in Yellowknife doing work he loves after being introduced as a summer student.

*"I loved what they were doing in the communities and I saw that they're making change. My main goal with work is just to make change in the community."*

Roache graduated and landed his dream job where he's had amazing experiences. *"Grise Fiord, Nunavut was my favorite place I've been to just because it's so far north. It took days to get there and six flights. Once we got there, you can tell it's very isolated. They don't get in a lot of contacts from the outside world, just because it's so far north and it's so expensive to get there,"* he recounted.

*"Me coming from a community and get my degree, and then bringing it back to work, it allows me to reach out to all the communities, not just my hometown and, and just be a role model and help change. The Sports Circle, that's their main focus, changing the communities."*

*Illustration by Shaikara David*

Getting to introduce sports to the community was exciting. *"Once I got there, and I started teaching these traditional games, they were really excited and they got into it. I was there for about four or five days, and by the third day, everyone was enjoying it and really got out of their shell and tried new things,"* Roache relayed.

Roach watched the community gain new skills, recalling, *"We hosted a little mini tournament and one of the games we threw was the one foot high kick. Some of these kids have never kicked before and they're kicking higher than me and I've been teaching it and it was nuts."*

He saw how those games brought people together. *"One of the guys' dads was kicking with his son. You just see that bond there, and they're both just kicking higher and higher and higher."* The organization left equipment behind so they could keep playing.

*"Growing up in a small town, you're faced with a lot of challenges such as drug use and just getting into trouble. I always found sports as a way to get out of it, hockey in the winter, soccer in the summer, softball, whatever you can do in a town of 400 people."*

Sports in that setting took creativity, like football in the snow and building a makeshift golf course with things found at a garbage dump. That improvised sports experience led to a passion for Roache.

He played on his first golf course in Fort Smith, then played every summer, got a membership and tried out for the university team where he was well coached. He learned to play and to make a difference.

*"Sports in the university were just a way to stay active, keep my mental health in check and engage with other people. My main focus for going to school was just to get a degree and make my way back up north and, and spread my knowledge with the communities."*

Leaving home to pursue his dreams was challenging. *"Being from a small community, you don't have access, you're not traveling for tournaments. You're not going on school trips. It's just so far north. Once you do leave, it's hard to break that shell. When I got to university, I wish someone told me to join all the clubs, go to all the events, make friends and just put yourself out there,"* he remembered.

His advice for youth leaving home is a message of hope: *"Don't be afraid that that's one thing that helped me, just stepping out of your shell and don't be afraid of anything. Stay active, go to the gym, join any team or rec league."*

*"Just know that your hometown, it's always your home. So when you go back, everyone welcomes you back and then they're really proud of you. Every time I go back, it still feels like home and I love going home."*

In his hometown, his mom inspired him. *"She was a cop back in the day with the strict rules, and she always encouraged staying in school. I made my way through school and she was always pushing me and always challenged me with everything,"* he said.

*"Going to university, my mom was always there anytime I needed help. I always looked up to her and see what she's done with the community of Délı̨nę. She's the band manager there, and she coordinates all the events. She's almost like the chief there. I just look up to her a lot as a role model."*

Roache knows his mom guided his journey, but she didn't do it alone. It takes a village to raise an athlete who would later come home to help create change. *"With the help of my friends and their support, they helped me get through everything I've gone through,"* Roache explained.

Pursuing sports and sharing them was a gamechanger for Carson Roache and for the communities where he's made an impact. Learning to innovate, persevere and have fun carried life lessons that would change not just his life but the lives of everyone his work has touched. Rooted in games, Carson Roache approaches each challenge like he's playing for keeps and that has made all the difference for himself and others.

*Watch the Future Pathways Fireside Chats video interview with Carson at https://www.firesidechats.ca/video/carson-roche*

Manufactured by Amazon.ca
Bolton, ON

40756711R00052